Robert Jennings

Horse-Training Made Easy

being a new and practical system

Robert Jennings

Horse-Training Made Easy
being a new and practical system

ISBN/EAN: 9783337391492

Printed in Europe, USA, Canada, Australia, Japan

Cover: Foto ©Lupo / pixelio.de

More available books at **www.hansebooks.com**

HORSE-TRAINING MADE EASY.

BEING

A NEW AND PRACTICAL SYSTEM OF TEACHING AND EDUCATING THE HORSE.

BEAUTIFULLY ILLUSTRATED WITH FORTY-FOUR ENGRAVINGS.

WHIP-TRAINING;

OR, HOW TO DRIVE WITHOUT REINS; HOW TO MAKE A HORSE TROT HONEST, &c.

By ROBERT JENNINGS,

VETERINARY SURGEON; PROFESSOR OF PATHOLOGY AND SURGERY IN THE
VETERINARY COLLEGE, PHILADELPHIA: LECTURER ON VETERINARY
MEDICINE IN THE AGRICULTURAL COLLEGE, PA.; AUTHOR OF
"THE HORSE AND HIS DISEASES," "CATTLE AND THEIR
DISEASES," "SHEEP, SWINE, AND POULTRY,"
ETC., ETC.

TO WHICH IS APPENDED,

AN ESSAY ON SHOEING;

ALSO,

THE SYMPTOMS AND TREATMENT OF THE VARIOUS
DISEASES OF THE HORSE, EMBRACING A FULL
AND COMPLETE HISTORY OF GLANDERS.

PHILADELPHIA:

PUBLISHED BY JOHN E. POTTER & CO.,
NO. 617 SANSOM STREET.

1866.

PREFACE.

THE art of training horses has, until within the last few years, been attended with much cruelty and bad management. The system known as Rarey's, though practised in this country for many years, was made popular. by Mr. J. S. Rarey, to whom we willingly accord all the credit which is justly due him. His success has given a new impulse to the inventive minds of horsemen; and, like almost all other discoveries, the original is lost sight of in the improvements which follow it. The Rarey system is one purely of subjugation and exhaustion; the spirit of the animal is thus often broken. On the contrary, our new system is one of education, embracing the practical portions of all the various systems known to man, from that of Sullivan the Irish whisperer, down to the more modern systems of the present day. The animal is first taught what is required of him, and, as soon as he is made to understand, he becomes a willing subject. To attempt to force him to do that which he does not comprehend, is to excite him to resistance, a circumstance always to be avoided; hence the many baulky, kicking, and otherwise unruly horses.

The Rarey system requires a man of nerve and determination to handle a horse successfully, which requisites few men possess. Ours enables a boy fifteen or sixteen years of age to handle, and break to harness, the wildest animal. Strength and courage are not essential; but patience, perseverance, and kindness are required. The man who is void of patience cannot control and win the confidence of his horse.

There is no other system known to man by which a horse can be trained to drive without bridle, bit, or reins, guided simply by motions of the whip. This principle is so simple, that any intelligent person can practise it successfully on any intelligent horse. To make a horse trot honest is also part of our system, it being original with us. We have

1* (5)

never known it fail. In March, 1865, I presented this subject to the consideration of the Philadelphia Society for Promoting Agriculture, and to the Philadelphia Riding Club, both of which institutions highly indorse it. Within the last year it has been greatly modified and improved, rendering it the most complete and practical system ever presented to the public.

To Messrs. Magner & Dudley, and to Messrs. Rockwell & Hurlburt, we acknowledge our indebtedness for valuable suggestions voluntarily offered us; also to Mr. J. E. Potter, Publisher, for the use of seven of our illustrations from the author's work, "The Horse and his Diseases."

The subject of shoeing horses, being one of great importance to horse-owners generally, has been duly considered. Twenty years' active practice as a veterinary surgeon, has enabled us to detect many errors in the present system of shoeing, and to suggest improvements which have proved of great service in remedying, in a measure, the evils of the present mode of shoeing. The bad effects of careless shoeing are fully demonstrated. We ask of the smith a fair and candid trial of our principle, and we will abide the issue.

The want of veterinary surgeons in most sections of the United States, and the urgent desire of many friends, has induced us to add to this work plain and simple directions for the treatment of the various diseases of that noble animal, including a full and complete history of that terrible and loathsome disease, *Glanders;* proving its contagious character and ready communication from horse to horse, and from horse to man. Under present circumstances, man cannot become too familiar with this dreadful disease.

This pamphlet was published by the author, and distributed gratuitously by the Philadelphia Agricultural Society, Pa., and the Burlington County Agricultural Society, N. J. The demand being several thousands more than the supply, is our motive in republishing it entire; all who wish it will now have an opportunity of obtaining it.

INDEX.

(7)

BIOGRAPHICAL NOTICE.

DR. ROBERT JENNINGS was born in the city of Philadelphia, on the 28th day of December, 1824, of English parents. As soon as he was able to comprehend anything, his love and admiration for the noblest of all the animal creation (excepting man himself), the horse, was the subject of general remark by his friends. As he grew in years, this passion became almost a mania. In the year 1832 his parents removed from Philadelphia to Mount Holly, where he had frequent opportunities of gratifying his passion. His daily haunts were the stables of the village. Young and sprightly animals were the chief objects of his attraction. In the year 1836 his father died. By this event he was thrown upon the world to seek his own living. Having obtained a situation for him as errand boy in a store, his mother sent him to the city; this did not suit his inclinations, and he soon changed his occupation, engaging in a printing office; the business still not suiting his tastes, he tried the confectionery business; still not satisfied, his uncle, Frederick Jennings, took him to his country seat, where he remained

(9)

until the following fall, when his uncle put him out to learn the coppersmithing business. Dissatisfied with this also, he turned his attention to the surgical instrument case making business, at which he remained until the spring of 1842. Becoming dissatisfied he went to New York, where he found employment for a time about the Bull's Head, riding and handling horses. In 1844 he took a trip with a drover to purchase horses, returning to New York the following spring. In the summer of 1845 he returned to the city of Philadelphia. He now turned his attention to the study of medicine, entering the office of Dr. James Bryan, late Prof. in the Geneva Medical College, N. Y., afterwards Prof. of Surgery in the Philadelphia Medical College. Soon after commencing his medical studies, his attention was called to a horse suffering from an attack of colic. Offering his services to treat it, which were accepted, the animal soon recovered under his fostering care. His preceptor soon discovered in his student, his fondness for the horse. Being naturally fond of that noble animal himself, frequent conversations occurred between the professor and his student respecting the diseases and suffering of this faithful, non-complaining servant of man. His thoughts now began to turn in a new channel, and, prompted by his preceptor, he applied himself to the study of veterinary medicine and surgery in connection with his other studies. There being no Veterinary Colleges in the United States, and not having the pecuniary means necessary for a voyage to

Europe, in order to gain a thorough veterinary education, his task was commenced with many difficulties surrounding him, which many less sanguine would have failed to combat. In 1852 Prof. Jas. Bryan, Gen. George Cadwalader, Prof. Wm. Gibson, M.D., John Phillips, M. D., Alfred L. Elwyn, M. D., Hon. Frederick Watts, Gen. George M. Keim, James Gowan, Esq., Hon. Geo. W. Woodward, Sketchley Morton, Esq, Alonzo Potter, D. D., and L. L. Ward, Esq., obtained a charter from the Pennsylvania State Legislature for a veterinary college, to be located in the city of Philadelphia. Robert Jennings having been the recipient of an honorary diploma from the board of directors, was placed at the head of the new institution. Not meeting with the encourage-ment which the enterprise deserved, the college project for the time was abandoned. Dr. R. J. removed from Philadelphia to Cleveland, in the spring of 1855, to fill the veterinary department in the Agricultural College of Ohio, situated at Cleveland Heights, Ohio City, under the charge of Prof. Norton S. Townsend, M. D. For three years he was ardently devoted to the interests of the college, without any pecuniary remuneration. The college failing to receive sufficient support from the farmers of the state, applied to the Legislature for an annual appropriation, which not being granted, the operations of the Institution were suspended. In the winter of 1858 Dr. R. Jennings returned to Philadelphia, and with the assistance of the Philadelphia Society for promoting Agriculture, and that of his friend Geo. W. Bowler, V. S. of Cincinnati, Ohio, commenced the first session of the Veterinary College of Philadelphia, with two students, Mr. W. A. Wisdom, of Delaware, and Jacob Dilts, of New Jersey. In 1860 he gave his first work to the world, "The Horse and his Diseases," which was very favourably received by the public. Soon after this book appeared, he was offered the position as lecturer on veterinary medicine and surgery in the Agricultural College, Centre county, Pennsylvania, which position he holds at the present time. In 1862 his second work was published, "Cattle and their Diseases," which also met a favourable reception at the hands of the public. In 1863 his third work on "Sheep, Swine, and, Poultry," made its appearance, meeting also with a favourable reception. During his professional career he has studied closely the disposition of the horse, finding it as variable as are those of man; and how to manage them successfully and easily has been his main object. A remarkable trait in his character, is his quick temper when dealing with men, and the complete control of that passion when handling horses, never having been known to become excited or angry with a horse under any circumstances.

HORSE-TRAINING MADE EASY.

HINTS ON TRAINING HORSES.

THE form, proportions, muscular powers, and swiftness of the horse, combined with its spirit, docility, and intelligence, expressly fit it for the use of man. It is alike serviceable for draft and the saddle. From its primeval nursery it has radiated in all directions; it has accompanied man in his wanderings over the world. To the industrious inhabitant of the thronged city, to the agriculturist, to the sportsman who follows the chase for pleasure, and to him who scours the plains in quest of prey, a "mighty hunter before the Lord," this noble, beautiful, but too often ill-treated creature, is either important or essential. It performs the drudgery of toilsome servitude; it draws the peaceful plough, and dashes on in battle amidst withering volleys of musketry and the clash of gleaming swords. Man owes a deep debt of gratitude to the horse, and is bound to acknowledge his sense of its value by humanity and kindness. In its natural state, the horse is gregarious; and in domestication it exhibits the same propensity to associate with its fellows. In the field they herd together, form

2 (13)

friendships, gambol with each other, and rush to
the fence to see a strange horse in the road,
saluting him with repeated neighings. So decided is the disposition of the horse to contract
friendship, that, when others of its species are
not accessible, it will attach itself to animals of a
different species. Many instances of mutual
attachment between dogs and horses have been
recorded. English Eclipse contracted a strong
friendship with a sheep. When kindly used, the
horse will demonstrate towards his master every
mark of submissive attachment. There are, it is
true, horses of a sullen, obstinate temper, which
the kindest treatment will not conciliate; but
these are exceptions to the general rule; many
horses, we may add, have their temper spoiled
by injudicious or wanton severity, in which case
it requires patience and perseverance to reclaim
them; but almost universally, where kindness
is shown to the horse, his attachment will be
secured.

In the tents of the Arabian, the mares with
their foals, and the masters with their families,
dwell all together; the master caresses his favorite mare, the children and the foal play together,
and the utmost confidence exists between them.
The quiet peaceful companionship of horses with
each other does not obtain among the stallions.
In a wild state, they have furious contests; and
in a domestic state, stallions, if at liberty, will
fight desperately with each other. Twenty years'
experience in active practice has afforded the

author very many opportunities of studying the
disposition of the horse, and how to manage it to
the best advantage has been his special study.
That the horse possesses more intelligence than
has been accredited to him is very evident from his
readiness to learn, when properly instructed. The
feats he is taught to perform in the "spectacles"
of the modern circus fully prove this. Knowledge
of time, and memory, are certainly possessed by
the horse, as a thousand instances will convince.
A horse accustomed to commence or leave off
work at a certain hour of the day, well knows
the respective periods. Well does the farmer's
team know the hour of release from labor, as is
shown by their actions when hearing the horn for
dinner. Taken to a distance from home, the
horse will return, finding his way during the
darkest night. The following, taken from an old
number of the London Penny Magazine, illustrates the love of the horse for its "old home :"—

"A short distance below Fort Erie, and about
a mile from where the river Niagara escapes over
a barrier of rocks from the depths of Lake Erie,
a ferry has long been established across the broad
and, there, exceedingly rapid river, the distance
from shore to shore being a little over one-third
of a mile. On the Canada side of the river is
the small village of Waterloo, and opposite
thereto, on the United States side, is the large
village of Black Rock, distant from the young and
flourishing city of Buffalo two miles. In com-
pleting the Erie Canal, a pier or dam was erected

up and down the river and opposite to Black Rock, at no great distance from the shore, for the purpose of raising the waters of the Niagara to such a height that they might be made to supply an adjoining section of the Erie Canal. This pier was and is a great obstruction to the ferry-boats; for, previous to its erection, passengers embarked from *terra firma* on one side of the river and were landed without any difficulty on the other; but after this dam was constructed it became necessary to employ two sets of boats, one to navigate the river, the other the basin, so that all the passengers, as well as goods and luggage, had to be landed upon this narrow wall and reshipped. Shortly after the erection of the pier-dam, a boat propelled by horses was established between this pier and the Canada shore. The boat belonged to persons connected with the ferry on the American side of the river; but, owing to the barrier formed by the pier, the horses employed on the boat were stabled at night in the village of Waterloo. I well recollect the first day this boat began to ply; for the introduction of a boat of that description in those days, was considered an event of some magnitude. The two horses (for the boat had but two) worked admirably, considering the very few lessons they had had previous to their introduction upon the main river. One of the horses employed on the new ferry-boat had once been a dapple gray, but at the period I am speaking of he had become white. He was still hale and hearty, for he had a kind and indulgent

master. The first evening after the horses had
been a short time in the stable, to which they
were strangers, they were brought for the purpose
of being watered at the river, the common cus-
tom of the place. The attendant was mounted
upon the bay horse, the white one was known
to be so gentle and docile that he was allowed to
drink where he pleased. I happened to be standing close by, in company with my friend W——n,
the ferry contractor, on the Canada side, and had
thus an opportunity of witnessing the whole proceeding of old Grizzle, the name that the white
horse still went by. The moment he got round
the corner of the building, so as to have a view
of his home on the opposite side of the river, he
stopped and gazed intently. He then advanced
to the brink of the river, then again stopped and
looked earnestly across for a short time, then
waded into the river until the water reached his
chest, drank a little, lifted his head, and, with
his lips closed and his eyes fixed upon some
object on the farther shore, remained for a short
time perfectly motionless. Apparently having
made up his mind to the task, he waded further
into the river until the water reached his ribs,
when off he shot into the deep water without
hesitation. The current being so strong and
rapid, the river boiling and turmoiling over a
rocky bed, at the rate of six miles an hour, it
was impossible for the courageous animal to keep
a direct course across, although he breasted the
waves heroically and swam with remarkable vigor.

2 *

Had he been able to steer his way directly across, the pier-wall would have proved an insurmountable barrier. As it was, the current forced him down below where the lower extremity of this long pier abuts upon an island, the shore of which being low and shelving, he was enabled to effect a landing with comparative ease. Having gained *terra firma*, he shook the water from his dripping flanks, when he plunged into the basin and soon regained his native shore. At the commencement of his voyage, his arched neck and withers were above the surface, but before he reached the island his head only was visible. He reached his own stable-door—that home for which he risked so much—to the no small astonishment of his owner. This unexpected visit made a favorable impression on his master, for he was heard to make a vow that if old Grizzle performed the feat a second time, for the future he should remain on his own side of the river, and never be sent to the mill again. Grizzle was sent back to work the boat the following day, but he embraced the first opportunity that occurred of escaping, and swam back the way he had done before. His owner, not being a person to break the promise he once made, never afterwards dispossessed him of the stall he had long been accustomed to, but treated him with marked kindness and attention."

Colonel Hamilton Smith, of the British Army, relates a case which proves the memory and attachment of the horse: "The Colonel had a

charger in his possession for two years, which he
left with the army, but which was brought back
and sold in London. About three years afterwards the Colonel chanced to travel up town, and
at a relay, on getting out of the mail, the off-
wheel horse attracted his attention; on going
near to examine it with more care he found the
animal recognised him, and testifying its satisfaction by rubbing its head against him, and
making every moment a little stamp with its forefeet, to the surprise of the coachman, who asked
if the horse was not an old acquaintance. It
was—it was his own old charger!"

" A lady, remarkable for benevolence to the
brute creation, observed from her garden-gate
one day a miserable horse, with the shoulder raw
and bleeding, attempting to graze upon an open
spot adjacent; having, by means of some bread,
coaxed the poor animal to the gate, she then
managed, with some assistance, to cover the
wound with adhesive plaster spread upon a piece
of soft leather. The man to whom the animal
belonged (one of those ignorant and careless
beings who are indifferent to the sufferings of
any but themselves) shortly afterwards led the
horse away. The next day, however, the horse
made his appearance again at the gate, over
which he put his head and gently neighed. On
looking at him it was found that the plaster was
removed, either by the animal's master, or by the
rubbing of the ill-made collar in which he worked.
The plaster was renewed. The third day he

appeared again, requiring the same attention, which he solicited in a similar manner. After this the plaster was allowed to remain, and the horse recovered; but ever after, when it saw its benefactress, it would immediately approach her, and by voice and action testify its sense of her kindness and notice. This anecdote, for the truth of which we can personally testify, proves how sensible the horse is of humane treatment, and how grateful for benefits bestowed."

Kind treatment and every care are due to an animal from whose services man derives such important benefits; but too often does man forget that he has a duty to perform, not only towards his fellow-man, but towards those domestic animals which Providence has intrusted to him for his welfare.

The apparatus used in training horses upon our new system are both cheap and simple. A common rope halter, a three or four ply cotton cord about twelve feet long, and a piece of line webbing, are all the implements required in training colts.

THE ROPE HALTER.

This should be made rather heavier and longer than those used upon broken horses, and so arranged, by tying a knot or otherwise, that it does not slip up so tightly as to pinch the animal's nose.

THE CORD.

This is nothing more than a three or four ply rope or cord. The cotton cord is much the best, as it works smoothly, and is much softer than any other. This cord is not a new feature in horse-training, as impostors would have you believe, it having been used many years by various tribes of Indians, Mexicans, &c. It is mentioned in the Veterinarian of London in 1828 as used by the North American Indians in sub-duing their horses: hence it is known as the Indian war bridle. A. H. Rockwell calls it the Yankee bridle, which claim is wrapped in some obscurity. The use of this simple arrangement is a powerful means of controlling horses, when properly used, otherwise it is more likely to do harm than good. To prepare the cord for use, tie a knot in each end, as seen in the engraving, then make a loop by doubling the cord and pass-ing the knot through, as represented by the engraving.

LOOPING THE CORD.

These loops should be at such distances from
the knot as will allow the cord to pass around the
neck at one end and the lower jaw at the other,
passing the knot through the loop from the opposite side of the loop to where it first passed through
in making the lap; this brings the thickness of the
cord in the centre of the loop.   By this means
safety is secured, the cord slipping easily through,
preventing the possibility of its getting fast, as
it would be likely to do if passed through the
loop from the same side it originally came
through.   The necessity of this arrangement will
be seen on applying the cord.   We have here
two principles involved : first, steady pressure
upon the lower jaw; second, friction in the mouth,

CORD APPLIED ON LOWER JAW.

CORD APPLIED ON NECK.

the one stationary in the mouth, the other slipping through it. The uses of these loops will be
explained in their proper places.

THE LINE WEBBING.

Take a piece of worsted webbing, such as is
used for driving-lines, divide it in two parts,
one piece of sufficient length to girt the body.
Make a loop in one end large enough for the
other end to pass through, so as, when adjusted,
it is sufficiently long to tie. The other part of the
web needs no loop. These two pieces of web are
used for various purposes, which will be explained
as we proceed.

HABITS OF THE HORSE.

Horses contract habits very easily when improperly managed, and transmit them to their offspring.

"'Tis easier to prevent than cure."

Every one at all conversant with the secrets of the stable know how readily habits are contracted, by the horse, and the difficulty in breaking up such habits when once contracted, by the ordinary methods. Many habits of the horse, in no way owe their origin to vice, yet are often as troublesome and dangerous as those which do.

KICKING IN THE STABLE.

To break up this dangerous habit, it is only necessary to place the animal in a stall closed at the head, or against a wall, so as to allow him no opportunity of jumping into or over the manger. Tie his head short, and suspend by a cord at either end, a bag of straw, hay, corn husks, or any soft material, so as to strike the hocks whenever the animal kicks. The bag rebounds, striking him upon the hocks : after several repetitions the animal is observed to stand and tremble; the bag .at this point is to be pulled upon one side so that he does not see it, and when the animal gets over his excitement try and induce him to kick. If you succeed, immediately let the bag go back to its former position. Two or three kicks will again quiet him, and he trembles as at first. Remove the bag, and when his excitement abates, try and induce him to kick again. By repeating this a few times the animal is thoroughly broken of the habit. Such horses are often broken of the habit of kicking in harness, as well as the stable, by the same means.

Kicking against the side of the stall is a serious evil. Capped hocks, and callous enlargements are frequently consequences of this habit; mares more frequently than geldings are subject to this vice. Particularly is this the case when placed beside other horses. Removal to a box stall, and left there unhaltered, will frequently break up the habit. When no such conveniences exist, a strap should be buckled around the leg above the hock, to which a club one and a half or two inches thick, and ten or twelve inches long, covered with a woollen cloth, or other soft material, so as not to hurt the animal, should be attached in such a

3

manner as to hang loosely against the shank bone; with this appendage the moment the animal kicks, this club punishes it by coming sharply in con- tact with the leg, but does not bruise it. The animal soon learns that by keeping the leg still he escapes the punishment which follows every effort to kick.

KICKING WHILE HARNESSING.

This habit is acquired by bad management in the early training of the horse; rough handling,. throwing the harness too quickly upon its back before it becomes thoroughly accustomed to its feel, are sufficient causes to produce this habit in the colt of a highly nervous temperament. The more quietly you go about such an animal, the more readily and willingly will he yield obedience to your desires. To break up this habit the cord is called into requisition; put the small loop over the under jaw, take your position upon the near side, opposite the shoulder, pass the cord over the neck from the off side, and carry it through the loop around the under jaw; now draw it up tightly and take a half-hitch, so as to keep the head in a confined position (represented in engraving), keep the cord in your hand, so in case of the animal rearing you can slip the hitch and let the head loose. You should then give him a few quick jerks; this diverts his attention; you now quietly take up the harness in your hands, and as quietly approach, and put it upon him. Should he attempt to kick, slip the loop as before, and give him a

few more sharp pulls upon the cord; this disconcerts him. Repeat this lesson a few times, and he
will soon learn to stand quiet while you are har-
nessing him.

KICKING WHILE GROOMING.

Horses of a high nervous temperament are
frequently addicted to this habit. This, like
kicking in harness, is brought on by careless or
rough handling. The cord here too is a powerful
instrument of control. Having secured the head,
use the brush and currycomb in the most gentle
manner for several days, particularly about such
parts as he manifests the most tenderness.

KICKING IN SINGLE HARNESS.

Previous to putting the animal in harness, take
the cord, put the small loop over the under jaw,
pass the rope over the neck from the off side and
through the small loop upon the near side;
give him a few quick pulls, which calls his attention to you. Put the harness upon him, having
a ring or loop upon the top of the bridle B and
a ring H secured to the back strap, about six
inches from the crouper. You now take a small bit,
attach to either ring a strong leathern strap about
half an inch wide, pass these straps A, A, A, A,
up over the face to the ring B in the bridle,
down through the terrets in the saddle, and back
through the ring H, then bring them down at
right angles, across the quarters and secure them
to the shafts on either side, in such a manner as

TWO METHODS FOR KICKING HORSES.

not to interfere with the animal in travelling. With this arrangement properly adjusted, the moment the horse attempts to kick, the strap is drawn tight over the quarters, at the same time it jerks up the head forcibly, punishing the animal at each attempt to kick.

KICKING IN DOUBLE HARNESS.

First use the cord upon the animal until he will yield his head on the slightest pull upon the cord; put on a halter, which should be a good strong leather one, having a strong lead, and ring F, (see Eng. p. 28), so adjusted as to slip under the girth. Have two strong straps with

STRAPS ON KICKING HORSE.

3 *

rings, on the plan of a dog collar. These are to be buckled around the leg above the hocks, D, D, a strong leathern strap fastened to the rings D, passing through the ring F, well secured, so as to be tense when the animal is standing square: now check him up, and he is ready to hitch up for the start. This arrangement does not interfere materially with his travelling, yet it reproves him whenever he attempts to kick, and he soon gives up the habit.

KICKING WHILE SHOEING.

CORD APPLIED ON LOWER JAW.

This, like most other habits, is brought on by bad management. The colt, upon first entering the shoeing shop, should be used with the greatest

gentleness and kindness. Any deviation from this
rule often causes the colt to resist all efforts to
shoe it. Particularly is this the case with the hind
feet. The habit once established, requires the
utmost care and perseverance to overcome the
evil. Ordinary cases of resistance while shoeing
may be brought to terms by the use of the cord
alone. To do this, put the small loop over the under
jaw, pass it over the neck, and through the loop
upon the opposite side, draw the cord tight, and
take a half-hitch; you will then take up the foot.
Should he resist, slip the hitch, and give him a
few quick jerks upon the cord, and then renew
the hitch. If he still refuses to let you have the
foot, repeat the operation. If he then resists,
put a collar around his neck, slip the long web
through the collar, carry it back, and around the
fetlock of the foot you wish to handle, bring it

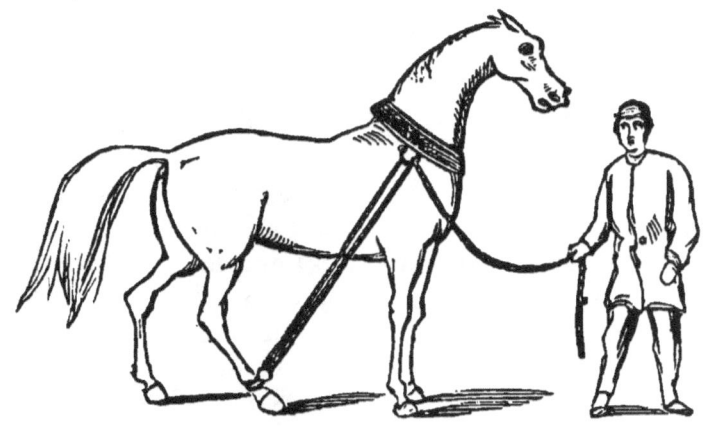

SIDE LINE.

back through the collar, holding the end in your right hand; now pull up the foot and hold it until he ceases to resist: then take the web in your hand close to the foot and pull the foot in different directions, until he ceases to resist your efforts; then caress him. Recollect, gentleness and kindness go a great way in gaining the confidence of the animal. When he gives you the foot readily, take a hammer and tap upon it very gently. If he resists, jerk him sharply a few times with the cord; if he still resists, remove the long web, then take a short hold upon the halter with your left hand, and with a quick motion catch the tail with the right hand, and swing him around a few times, by quickly bringing the head towards you. This so disconcerts him that he usually yields the foot without further resistance. For safety it is always better to put the web on again for one or two handlings. Properly managed you will seldom fail in breaking up this habit in from four to six days.

HORSES UGLY TO SHOE IN FRONT.

Take the short web, put it on the foot (at the fetlock) you wish to handle, pass it over the back from the opposite side; now pull the foot up and hold it there until the animal ceases his efforts to get it away, then tap lightly with a hammer upon the foot, increasing the force of the blow gradually, until he will allow you to strike upon the foot as hard as may be necessary; then let the foot down, pick it up with the hand; if he resists, draw it up again with the web; and so repeat until he yields it readily and willingly. Usually the animal submits his foot in a very short time, unless he becomes excited by rough usage.

THE LONG FOOT-STRAP.

STRIKING.

Some horses have an ugly practice of striking with their front feet. To break up this habit take the cord, put the small end in the mouth, and jerk him from one side to the other; he will try to strike you, but he fails to do so if you give him sufficient length of cord; he soon finds he is overmatched, and yields to you readily. By using the long foot-strap or web, placed around the near forefoot, then passed under the girth, and carried back, having an assistant at the animal's head to lead him, as soon as he steps, pull up the foot, let it drop and pull it up again at

the next effort to step or strike. This teaches
him that he cannot use the foot as he would like,
and he ceases to make the effort.

BAULKING.

This is the most aggravating of all the habits
to which the horse is subject; it tries the patience
of man to the utmost; yet, by patience and perseverance, with proper management, even this
habit can be broken up. It is rarely we find a
baulky horse which is not a good one. They are
usually very hardy, high-spirited, quick of com-
prehension, and of a strong nervous temperament.
They resist because we have failed to make them
understand what we require of them, or it may
occur from overloading, sore shoulders, or work-
ing until tired out. Particularly is this the case
with young animals. To whip under such circumstances only excites them to more determined
resistance. On the first attempt of your horse
to baulk, get out of the wagon, pat him upon the
neck, examine the harness carefully, first upon
one side then upon the other, speaking encouragingly to the animal while doing so; then jump
in the wagon and give the word to go; generally
he will obey; if he refuse to do so, take him
out of the shafts, put up the traces so that they
do not drag upon the ground, then take him by
the head and tail, reel him until he is almost
ready to fall, then hook him up again, and give
him the word to go; this rarely fails, it takes that
sullen spirit out of them, and they start at the

3 *

word. I have failed but once in handling baulky horses, though I have handled a large number of them. By repeating the same operation every day for a week, usually breaks up this most perplexing habit thoroughly and permanently. Another method which often proves successful, is to tie the tail of the horse fast to the shaft-bar, unloose the traces, securing them so that they will not get under his feet. Now start him up; as soon as he finds his tail fast he will pull the wagon by that appendage; repeating this a few times will often cure the habit. Another method still will sometimes prove successful: instead of tying the tail to the shaft-bar, take it between the hind-legs, having a cord secured to the end, and tie it to the saddle-girth; this will often answer the same purpose.

SHYING HORSES.

. Those who are in the habit of riding or driving along frequented roads, or through thickly populated cities, can best estimate the inconvenience, annoyance, and constant apprehension occasioned by a shying horse. While travelling along with an air of the greatest unconcern, all in an instant, planting himself in an attitude of affright, he comes to a dead stop, or flies the road. Of the sensation of the animal at such a time, we will not venture a description, but we know by experience what those of the driver or rider are. Shying in horses is no doubt the off-spring of fear. Fear is the emotion excited by suspicion, apprehension, appearance or approach of danger. This may be denominated *native timidity*, giving rise to that kind of shyness with which colts, and young animals generally, are endowed. There is another kind of shyness which we may denominate acquired. To illustrate, a colt is naturally shy at any object of imposing appearance, either novel or strange to him. On the other hand, he beholds an object that is familiar to him, which he associates with some former suffering. We do not mean to assert that these manifestations of fear are alike, further than that they arise from the impressions made upon the brain, a dread or consciousness of danger, in the one case acquired, in the other congenital. Shyness may be attributed to a third cause, imperfect vision. A horse whose eyesight is imperfect is apt to shy at objects in consequence of not seeing them properly. The disposition to shy arising from either of the above causes, is often increased by the acts of the driver; for instance (a very common one), a man is driving a young horse upon the road, he meets an object of fear to the animal, and, as he approaches it, starts suddenly out of the road, his driver instantly commences a round of castigation with the whip, in which he persists until the horse, as well as himself, have lost their temper, and then, while one whips, the other jumps, plunges, frets, &c. The next object of fear the animal meets recalls the whipping previously inflicted upon him. and associates it with the object he fears, shies, and starts with even more alarm than before, sometimes attempting to run away. Gentleness and persuasion are the best means of breaking up this habit; let the animal stand and look at the object he fears, speak to him encouragingly, and gradually he will approach it. After he has passed it, turn him around, passing the object slowly several .times, and his fear vanishes. By thus gently managing him, he soon places confidence in you, and a gentle word from the driver will induce him to move on by the object. It is an· old saying, that the most effectual way to make a cowardly dog fight is to put him in front of his antagonist, in such a way that he cannot retreat; but we never heard any one recommend that he be whipped at the same time; yet we whip a horse for being afraid to do that which we desire him to do. Reason and experience both forbid the practice. It is our duty to act mercifully towards an animal so noble, so beautiful, and so useful to man. Contemptible indeed is that being who disregards the plaintive murmurs and ineffectual resistance of the poor beast which chance has thrown into his possession.

WEAVING.

This is an unsightly habit, but not of so much consequence as either of the foregoing. It consists in the animal moving his head and fore-quarters in quick succession from one side of the stall to the other, like the action of a weaver's shuttle, or like the hyena in his cage. The ani-

3

mal stands with his forefeet wide apart, hence the motion of the animal throws the weight of its body alternately upon the inside of each fore-foot. The effect of this habit is to turn the inside quarter of the feet downwards and inwards at the heel, forming, as it were, a kind of club-foot. This habit indicates a restless disposition, expressing impatience at being tied up. To break up the habit, it is only necessary to turn the animal loose into a box-stall.

CRIBBING MUZZLE.

CRIBBING.

This is a very disagreeable habit, to say the least, but not so serious as it is often represented. The effects of an inveterate crib-biting horse are

plainly perceptible upon the incisor (nippers)
teeth. The cribbing muzzle is the best means
of breaking up the habit. See Jennings on
"The Horse and his Diseases."

BITING HORSES.

This is a hateful habit, or, more properly, a
vice of the worst kind. It is sometimes acquired
from foolishly teasing the animal in the stable by
mischievous boys. Love of mischief is a propensity too easily acquired, and often becomes a
confirmed vice; particularly is this the case with
biting horses. Last spring (1865) my advice
was asked regarding a horse which had always
been known as a remarkably good dispositioned
animal, but, some four or five months previous,
some boys amused themselves by teasing him.
He soon acquired the habit of biting, and, almost
simultaneously, that of striking. Regarding the
former vice—one of the most dangerous and the
most difficult of all vices to break up—I advised
castration; the owner approving, I operated upon
him on the spot. Instead of curing the habit,
he from this time became notoriously vicious, two
men narrowly escaping with their lives from the
infuriated animal. He finally became so confirmed in his vicious propensities, it was worth a
man's life to approach him. The owner, whose
name I omit by request, called upon me to handle
this animal, which I did on the sixth day of Oc-
tober, 1865, at his residence, near Princeton,
New Jersey. My efforts were attended with

entire success. I first drew his head down close to the manger from an opening in the partition, having his head well secured. The stable-door was thrown open. I then approached his head cautiously, and put my rope halter upon him. I now tied a knot in his tail, slipped the halter lead through the hair above the knot, drew the lead up as far as possible, so as to draw the head to one side, and tied the halter lead by a half-hitch to the tail; this prevented the animal going in a straight line, and enabled me to keep out of his way. I now slipped the head-halter, previously upon him, and drove him out of the stable. The moment he gained the yard, I was after him, tickling him upon the hind-legs with a whip. This set him wild with rage, and caused him to move in a circular direction quite rapidly. I kept up this action until he began to stagger; I quickly caught the halter at the head to prevent his falling, and, before he had time to recover himself, I tightened the halter so as to bring the head and tail nearer together. I again started him, he reeled more rapidly, and came near falling; I caught the end of the halter, slipped the hitch, and, before he had time to recover, I had the small end of the cord nicely adjusted in his mouth. I then commenced to pull him right and left, and in a few minutes he was as quiet as a lamb, following me readily in any direction. He was handled by the owner in the same manner for several days. I recently heard from him; he remained perfectly tractable. My friend Mr. E.

C. Dudley, of the firm of Magner & Dudley horse trainers, accompanied me to see this horse.

RUNNING AWAY.

Some horses, of an excitable or headstrong disposition, will make frequent efforts to get away with his driver, and, when once he succeeds, he is very apt to try it over again. Such animals must be trained upon the mouth. To do this effectually, take the cord, using the large loop, over the neck, placing the cord in the mouth, and back through the loop. You now pull

TEMPERING THE MOUTH.

quickly and sharply upon the cord, this sets the horse back, and causes the mouth to become

tender.   You then go behind him, pulling quick
upon the cord.   Handle him several times in
this way before putting him in harness; he soon
yields promptly to the slightest pull upon the
cord.   You may now harness him up; and, as a
matter of safety, put the long web around the
near foot, and give it in charge of an assistant.
Let him take it in the buggy.   With him, you

TAKING UP THE FOOT.

start on your journey; if the animal attempts to
run, pull upon the lines, and he will generally
come down to his usual gait.   Should he not
obey this gentle warning, let your assistant take
up his foot by pulling the web.   This throws him
upon three feet, and prevents his running.
Another method, more convenient and equally

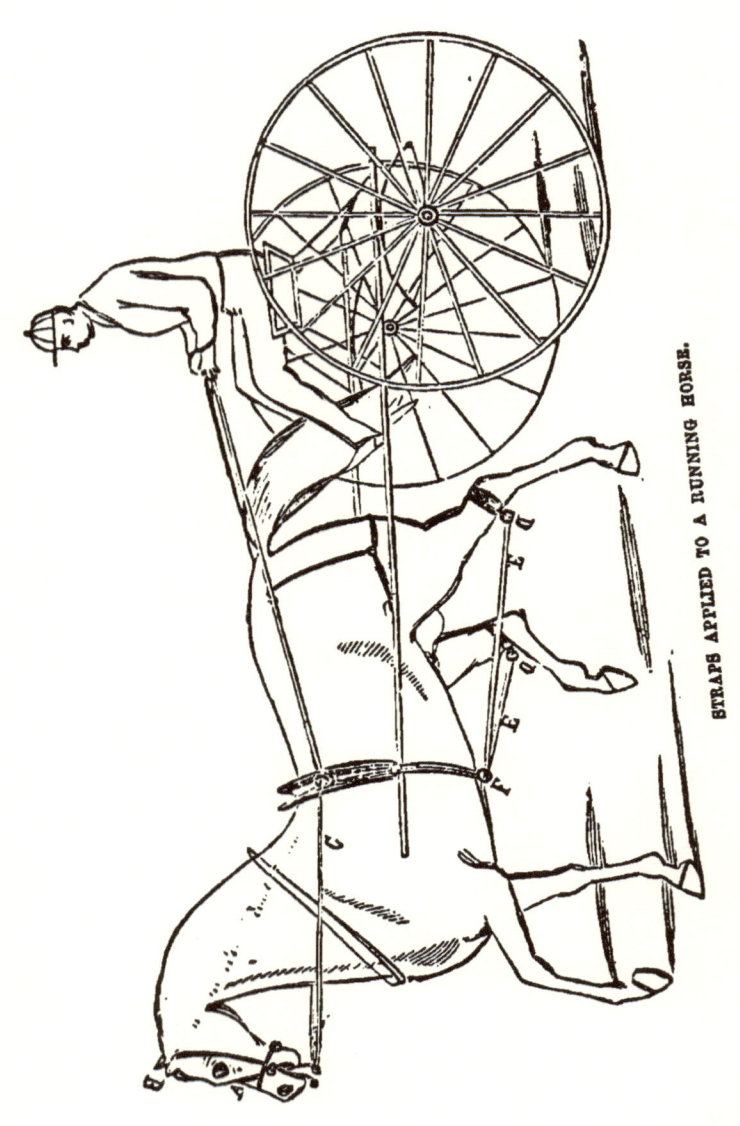

STRAPS APPLIED TO A RUNNING HORSE.

effectual, is the apparatus used for kicking horses, with this difference, instead of fastening the ring

STRAPS ON KICKING HORSE.

which passes under the girth to the halter, secure it to the collar (see Eng. p. 46). With this arrangement upon him, a horse cannot run. It is not necessary to have the straps as heavy as for a kicking horse.

REFUSING TO STAND WHILE GETTING INTO A CARRIAGE.

This habit is very easily broken up. Use the cord upon the mouth, have it long enough to

CONTROLLING THE MOUTH.

take in your hand; when entering the carriage, if the horse starts, jerk lightly upon the cord; if he does not obey, bring him back forcibly by a quick, strong jerk on the cord. This soon teaches him to stand until you are ready for him to start.

HARD PULLERS, OR LUGGERS ON THE BIT.

To break up this habit, use the cord in the same manner as upon a runaway horse, or have a pair of straps about twelve inches long, with a ring at one end and a buckle at the other; pass these straps through the ring of the bit on either side, carry them up on the side of the face, and buckle to the head-piece of the bridle, which must be a strong one; buckle the lines to the rings on these straps, instead of the rings in the bit. This forms a gag, similar to the French twitch gag, and is a powerful means of controlling the mouth of a hard-pulling horse.

UGLY TO BRIDLE.

Some horses are ugly to bridle from having been knocked or roughly handled about the head. Horses are occasionally troubled with sore ears, or have some tenderness about the mouth or head. Such animals refuse to be bridled from fear of being hurt. Nothing but kindness and careful

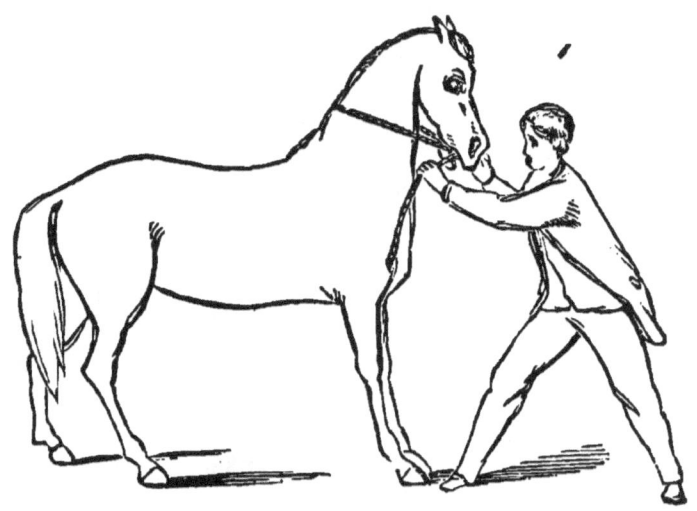

KEEPING THE HEAD DOWN.

5

handling will accomplish our purpose in such
cases. Where the habit arises from previous
injury or ugliness of disposition, take the cord,
put the small end into the mouth, draw it tightly,
and take a half-hitch. This confines the head,
preventing the animal from raising it. In this
position, the horse will allow you to put on and
take off the bridle at pleasure. After putting it
on and removing it several times, loosen up the
cord, and repeat the bridling; every time the
animal resists, draw the cord tightly; on the
contrary, when he yields, caress him; you thus
gain his confidence.

LOLLING THE TONGUE.

Some horses have a habit of carrying the
tongue out of one side of the mouth. This is
generally confined to narrow-jawed horses, the
space between the molar teeth being too narrow to
contain the tongue in the mouth when the bit
presses upon it, without coming in contact with
the edges of the molar teeth, to prevent which
the tongue is thrown out over the bit and hangs
frcm one side of the mouth. To remedy this
defect, take a common bar bit, drill a hole on
either side, about three-quarters of an inch from
the centre of the bit, from the upper surface;
then take a piece of sole leather, four inches
long and two inches wide, sprinkle it over with
pulverized rosin and burn it into the leather, this
renders it proof against the action of the saliva

in the mouth; now drill two holes in the centre
of the leather corresponding to those in the bit,
and secure both together by rivets, so that the
leather extends two inches above the bit and two
inches below it; this, put into the mouth, keeps
the tongue down clear of the molar teeth, and
prevents the animal getting it over the bit. A
horse which lolls the tongue should never be
driven with a snaffle bit; a bar bit is always
preferable.

HUGGING THE POLE.

This is a great annoyance to the other horse,
and he will probably learn to do the same thing,
not from imitation, but from leaning inwards so
as to enable him to stand against the other leaning on him. I have seen a pair of horses thus
going, each leaning on the other, rendering it
extremely dangerous in frosty weather, or where
the road from any cause may be slippery. This
habit may be broken up by securing a piece of
sole leather to the pole upon the side where the
animal leans, having a number of tacks driven
through it in such a manner as to protrude from
the leather towards the horse. The moment he
attempts to hug the pole, the tacks prick him,
and he leaves it in a moment and takes his proper
position. He makes but few efforts after the first
punishment; a few days' driving in this manner,
usually cures him of the habit.

TO MAKE A HORSE TROT HONEST.

Many horses show speed when they strike their gait, but do not hold it long. This, in many instances, arises from too much anxiety on the part of the driver, forcing the horse off his feet. This is a great source of annoyance to the owners, who in many instances have built their hopes very highly upon the great speed of their favorite nag. But how often are they doomed to disappointment! the animal is beaten by those of far less speed, simply because he breaks up badly. To prevent this habit in horses, requires some degree of patience and good management on the part of the trainer. The apparatus used upon this occasion is a similar one to that used for kicking horses. The straps *e e* are the same; the halter lead, however, is not required; use instead a strap passed through the collar; the choke-strap will answer the purpose, if not too long; to this strap secure the ring *f*, pass the strap *e e* through the ring *f*, and buckle the straps *d d* above the hocks. We are now ready to drive the horse, going off on a moderate gait, that he may become familiar with the feel of the straps prior to urging him. As he moves, the strap *e e* slips through the ring *f*, allowing the animal to move without restraint as long as the legs move alternately, as they do in the trot or pace; but the instant he attempts to change his gait, he then meets the check which the straps give him; he cannot move them together as he does in the run, the straps

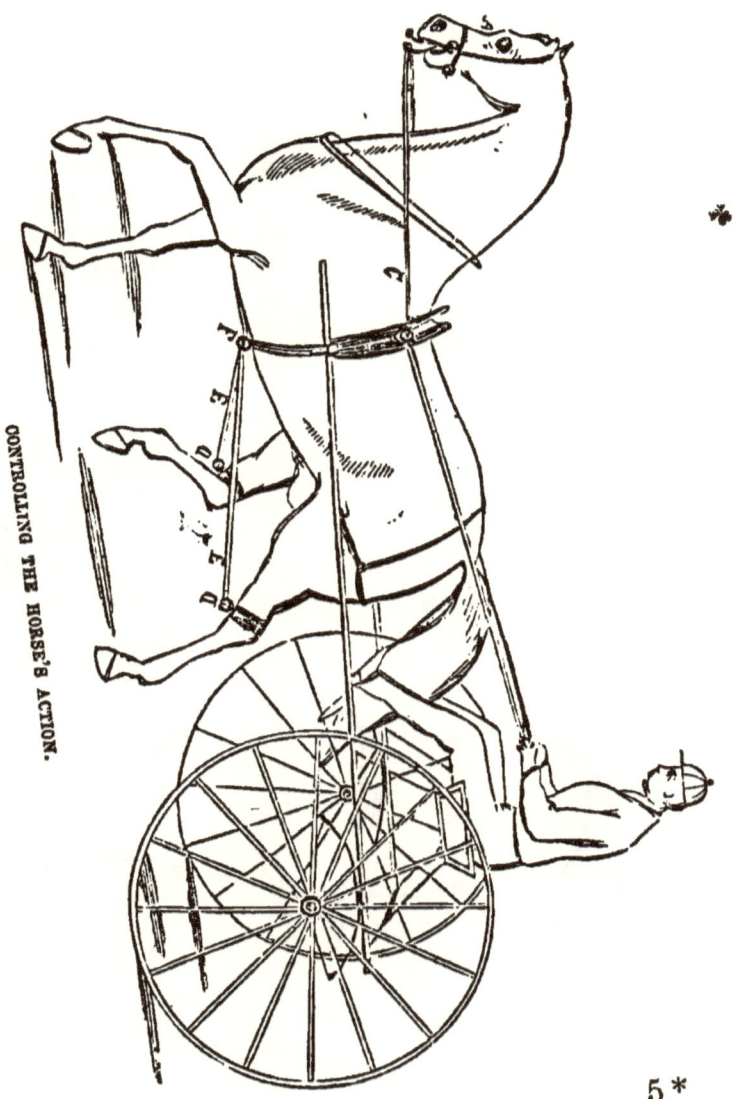

CONTROLLING THE HORSE'S ACTION.

5 *

preventing both legs going back at the same time. After he has made a few attempts to break up and fails, he becomes gradually more steady. We may then urge him to the top of his speed without his making any effort to go up. Drive him every day with this arrangement for three or four weeks, and by that time he will, as a general thing, trot perfectly honest and remain so.

HALTER PULLING.

This is a bad habit, often contracted by bad management on the part of those having the care of young animals. It is one, however, with care the a little patience, easily broken up. For this purpose we use an ordinary rope halter, with a

TO PREVENT HALTER PULLING.

PULLING ON THE HALTER.

lead long enough to pass through the halter-
ring then back between the forelegs and under a
surcingle, and tie with a slip-knot to one of the
hind feet, be careful that the halter ring is strong
enough to resist the pull; now put him back,
and as he pulls, the halter draws both ways, upon
the head and on the hind foot; he rarely makes
more than two or three attempts to pull back.
You may now approach him, and try your best
to set him back, whip him over the nose, throw
your hat in his face, a buffalo, or any other object
which he may fear, and all will fail to set him
back; repeat this a few times, and he will give

up the habit. When in harness it is not safe to hitch him thus, as it gives him an opportunity to pull himself down; it is therefore better to tie the halter around the body, back of the shoulders, instead of tying it to the foot; if he pulls now, he pulls against his fore-arms, but it does not take him off his feet. Another plan is to tie a knot in the tail so that it will not slip, then divide the hairs in the middle above the knot, and pass the end of the halter through the opening and tie it, so that when he pulls it brings the tail between the hind legs; thus fixed, he pulls upon his head and tail. Either of these plans will effectually break up the habit.

OBJECTS OF FEAR.

Some horses are naturally far more timid than others, and take alarm at objects which in others produce no fear. We have seen horses dreadfully agitated during a thunder-storm; while, on the contrary, we have observed some apparently indifferent to the flashes and roar. In cases where horses are in stables on fire, fear appears to paralyze their powers, so that it is very difficult to rescue them, unless they be first blindfolded, which should always be done. Professor Rodet relates several curious cases of this character: "In 1806, during the campaign of Austerlitz, a Piedmontese officer possessed a beautiful, and in other respects, a most serviceable mare, but which one peculiarity rendered at times exceedingly

dangerous for the saddle : she had a decided
aversion for paper, which she immediately recognised the moment she saw it.   The effect
produced by the sight or sound of it was so
prompt and so violent, that, in many cases, she
unhorsed her rider; and in one case, his foot
being entangled in the stirrup, she dragged him
a considerable way over a stony road.   In other
respects, this mare had not the slightest fear of
objects that would terrify most horses.   She
regarded not the music of the band, the whistling
of the balls, the roaring of the cannon, the fire
of the bivouacs, or the glittering of arms.   The
confusion and noise of an engagement made no
impression upon her; the sight of no other white
object affected her; no other sound was regarded; .
the view or the rustling of paper alone aroused
her to madness.   A mare belonged to the Guard
Royal from 1816 to 1821.   She was perfectly
manageable, and betrayed no antipathy to the
human being nor to other animals, nor to horses,
except they were of a light gray color; but the
moment she saw a gray horse, she rushed upon
it and attacked it with the greatest fury.   It was
the same at all times and everywhere.   She was
all that could be wished on the parade, on the
route, in action, and in the stable; but such
was her hatred towards gray or white horses,
that it was dangerous to place them in the same
stable with her at whatever distance.   If she
once caught a glimpse of one, whether horse or
mare, she rested not until she had thrown her

rider or broken her halter, and then she rushed upon it with the greatest fury, and bit it in a thousand places. She generally, however, seized the animal by the head or throat and held it so fast that she would suffocate it if it were not promptly released from her bite. No other white body appeared to make the least impression on her. A mare belonging to the fifth squadron hussars feared, on the contrary, all white inanimate objects, such as white mantles or cloaks, and particularly white plumes. When any of these white bodies, and especially in motion, were suddenly perceived, if they were of any magnitude and their motion was rapid, she was in a dreadful fright, and strove to escape; but if they were of no great size, and moved more gently, she rushed furiously upon them, struck at them with her forefeet, and endeavored to tear them with her teeth. No other colors produced the slightest effect upon her, nor did the appearance, however sudden, of white horses or dogs of the same color; but if a white plume waved, or a white sheet of paper floated by her, her fear or rage was ungovernable."

Professor Rodet regards these as cases of true monomania. It is remarkable that in each instance the subject of this singular frenzy was a mare. Some animals are very much alarmed at the sight of a buffalo-robe, an umbrella, &c. To break up these habits requires more care than is usually required for other habits. Take the cord, put the small loop in the mouth, place the object

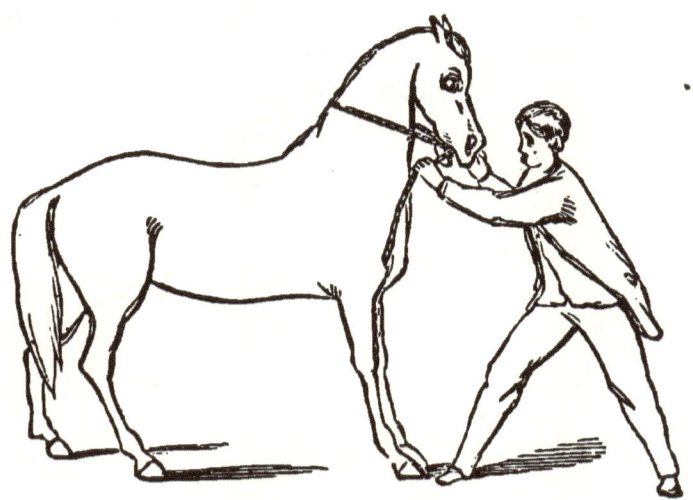

TEACHING THE HORSE TO STAND.

of fear at a distance, lead the animal as near it
as possible, have an assistant to raise it off the
ground; if the animal attempts to get away from
it, jerk him sharply from side to side a few times,
then have your assistant approach with the object
of fear very slowly, and each time the animal flies
from it, jerk him as before, and so repeat until
he will allow you to approach near enough to rub
him on the nose. If it is a buffalo-robe, stroke
him upon the neck, gradually put it on his back,
take it off and put it on again; repeat until he
stands perfectly quiet; now approach him from
another direction, he now starts up again as at
first, jerk him in the same manner, and repeat
every day until he will allow you to approach

him from any direction. A week or ten days is sufficient to break up the habit thoroughly, if properly managed.

Another very good method is the halter so arranged as for halter pulling. Having the

THE HALTER PULLER.

animal ready, take the buffalo-robe on your arm, approach as near as possible without causing the horse to pull back, stand a moment, and, when the animal gets over the temporary excitement, gradually approach it; the horse now pulls upon the halter, and comes back to his proper place; in five minutes, generally, he will stand and allow you to put the buffalo on him in any way you please. Occasionally we find a case

TRYING TO GET AWAY.

that does not yield readily.   Under such circumstances, the cord, small end, should be applied in
addition to the halter.   Now approach him gradually; if he does not stand quietly, give him a
quick, sharp pull upon the cord.   Take the cord
off, leaving the halter upon him; lay the buffalo
on the floor before the animal, and leave him to
examine it for an hour or two; now hang it over
the back part of the manger, and leave him again
in the same manner; then hang it up in the en-
try before him, so that he can view it at a short
distance, then change its position, hang it up
behind him; finally you may put it over his back,

6

and secure it with a surcingle. By changing it in this manner, he becomes familiar with its appearance in any position. A horse will often see an object in one position and not notice it; but place the same object in a different position, and the animal becomes alarmed. One day usually is sufficient to break up this habit, completely and thoroughly.

HALTERING THE COLT.

To do this without the colt offering resistance, it is necessary to drive him into a cow-stall or other convenient place. You will now, with your hand if you can reach him, otherwise with a stick of sufficient length, touch him gently upon the quarter; this will cause him to start up, and perhaps to turn around in the stall. Do not attempt to prevent his doing so, or you increase his excitement, which at all times should be carefully avoided. You will then repeat the operation, and in a few minutes he will stand quietly and allow you to stroke him with your hand, or stick; gradually pass the hand or stick up over his back, as he will bear it, until you reach his head; if he attempts to get away, do not try to prevent his doing so, as you will fail in the attempt. As soon as he will allow you to stroke his head, take up an ordinary rope halter, such as are used upon colts, pull out the lead so as to form a good sized loop, place it on the end of a stick, and hold it towards him; let him smell ·

HALTERING THE COLT.

it, and, as he does so, let his nose pass through the loop; raise the upper part of the halter over his head, then turn the stick and the halter will fall back of the colt's ears. Slip up the lead and you have him fast; now place the lead over his neck and secure it by a slip-knot, so as to keep him from treading on it. Open the stall-door and let him go out. Now drive him into a carriage-house, or some other suitable place, not more than twenty-five or thirty feet square; you then approach him; he runs to a corner; take a pole six or eight feet long, and commence as before by touching him on the quarter; and as the pole approaches the neck, close up gradually until you can put your hand upon him; you will then dispense with the pole, slip the knot in the halter, and remove the lead from his neck. You now have one end of the halter, the colt the other; you want to teach him to lead; you take your position a little quartering from his body, and nearly opposite his shoulder. You say, Come here, sir; your colt pays no attention to your command, because he does not understand you; give the halter a quick, sharp pull, which brings the colt towards you. The instant you pull, let the halter slack, this prevents him from pulling back: if you keep your lead tight, he learns that he is fast, and he will pull in spite of all your efforts to prevent his doing so; repeat this operation several times, always using the words Come here, your colt will soon learn to follow you in the one direction. You then go to the opposite side and teach him to follow in the same manner; he must be handled from both sides, or he will obey but one. He now follows to the right or left. You want him to go forwards; take your position a little to one side, but slightly in advance of his head; give your halter a sharp, quick pull, and as your colt steps forward, stop and caress him; repeat this a few times, and he will follow you in any direction.

HITCHING THE COLT IN THE STABLE.

Lead him into an ordinary stall four and a half feet wide, having previously fitted a movable bar at the back of the stall about three feet and a half from the floor, or, if more convenient, a good strong rope, well secured, will answer the purpose—let it be about the same distance from the floor. After leading the colt into the stall, put up this bar or rope, and then tie the colt to the manger-ring; if you do so at first, he will in all probability run back before you can have the bar or rope secured in their place; and then the halter gives way, and you have taught the colt the first lesson in halter-pulling, which under all circumstances should be carefully avoided. In taking the colt out of the stable the same precaution must be used. Untie the halter before removing the bar or rope. Continue this precaution for about ten days or two weeks, and by that time, as a general rule, the colt will stand hitched anywhere.

TRAINING COLTS TO HARNESS.

To break a colt successfully, requires a man who has inexhaustible patience, great presence of mind, strong nerve, &c., in a word, a man who can control himself, can train a horse to harness, so as to prevent their contracting any bad habits. With such indispensable attributes and proper appliances, a man of ordinary intelligence can train a horse to harness without accident to the animal, himself, or others. Always train a colt with an open bridle, so that he may see exactly what you are doing: using the blind bridle prevents the animal from seeing your movements,

6 *

and unless you use great care and judgment, you are apt to alarm the colt from the least misplaced movement. Let a man recollect how surprised, and in some cases alarmed, he feels on anything touching him behind. The same is the case with the horse where he does not see the object. We may say it was only the end of the trace that touched him; how is he to know this if he does not see it? A man standing in the street would turn as quickly round if a harmless sheep touched him, as if it were some more formidable animal. We must, therefore, be careful not to alarm or confuse the horse. Do everything in the most gentle and persuasive manner; if you do anything which frightens your colt, he never forgets it. Take time, and teach each point in training thoroughly; remember, that which is done hurriedly, is done badly.

HARNESSING.

Horses, whether young or old, sometimes have an aversion to going in harness; such animals show their unwillingness by kicking, baulking, rearing, running back, or, perhaps, running away. To prevent such habits being developed, take the colt, after being thoroughly halter-broken, by the head and tail, reel him a few times, and you can put the harness upon him; by this means you disconcert him, he will not then resist you; place him in the stable with the harness upon him, and leave him there a few hours, so that he may become accustomed to it. Then bring him out, take the lines behind him, having an assistant at his head, and teach him thoroughly the use of the reins, turning him to the right and to the left, until he will obey the slightest pull upon the reins; after having him so that he will start at the word, turn to the right or to the left, by a pull upon the line; he is ready for the word

WHOA.

This is the most important word used in horse-training; it is our safeguard in case of accident; the animal, therefore, should learn its meaning thoroughly. To prevent confusion in his mind, the word should never be used out of its proper place. If we approach a horse standing quietly

WHOA.

in the stable, we should never use the word *whoa*,
though it is very generally used on such occasions. Use instead the words Get over, Go over,
Quietly, my pretty boy, or any other word you
please, to make the animal aware of your presence; but under no circumstances use the word
whoa, except when the animal is in motion, and
you want him to stop. In order to properly
teach him the meaning of the word *whoa*, put
the long web around the near fore-foot, pass it
under the girth, and as the animal walks along,
pull up the foot, at the same time say *whoa;* by
repeating this, you will soon see him raise the
foot when the word is given, even though the
web is not pulled upon. Horses thus trained are
safe in case a rein or bit should break, as they
will generally stop at the word, under almost any
circumstances. A friend of mine trained his
horse to stop by simply catching hold of the tail.
You are now ready for

LEARNING TO BACK.

Put the cord upon the horse, using the small
loop; draw it up with a steady pull,—this brings
the animal's nose towards his body. Keep a
firm hold upon the cord until he steps back
a little, using at the same time the word back,
then caress him; you thus teach him that he
has done exactly what you wished him to do;
then repeat caressing him each time he obeys.
Care must be used not to excite the colt too

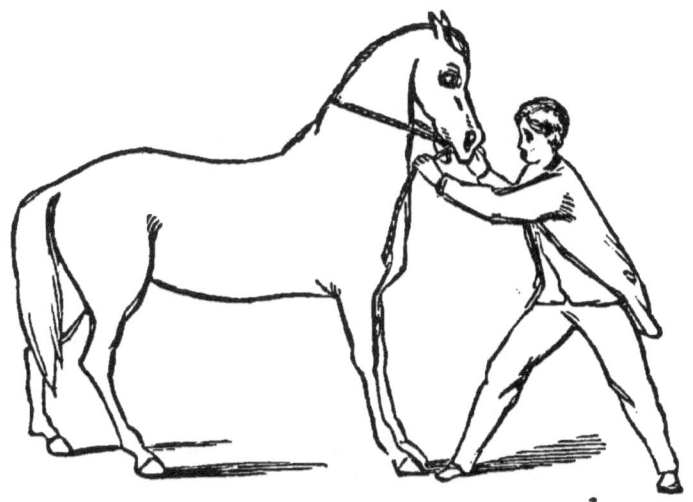

LEARNING TO BACK.

much or you will have him resist you; therefore, do not continue your lesson more than five or ten minutes at any one time; on repeating the lesson a few hours later, the animal will usually yield and back freely. Now try him with the line alone; if he obeys, you may remove the cord altogether. Occasionally, we find an animal which will not yield to this treatment; we then take the short web, put it around the near fore foot, carry it over the back from the off-side, have a bridle upon the animal, take hold of it close to the bit with your left hand on the near side, having the web in the right hand, with which bring up the near fore foot, holding it up by the web, now press backwards upon the bit, this

brings the body back, and as it does so, let the
foot fall; the toe strikes the ground some fifteen
or eighteen inches behind the opposite foot, and
as it does so, the off-foot comes back to the same
point. By repeating this lesson, we teach any
horse to back, however obstinate he may be. I
have never known a single instance where it
failed.

HITCHING TO THE WAGON.

In hitching up a colt to the wagon for the first
time, it is always better that you put him along-
side of a steady, well-broken horse; if you have
no opportunity of doing this, let him become
perfectly familiar with the wagon before hitching
him up single; lead him up to the wagon in the
shafts of which you intend putting him; let him
examine it carefully; raise the shafts up and
down in his presence, so as to get him familiar
with the motion; if it be a top-buggy, raise and
lower the top; should he behave badly, put the
cord upon him, using the small end; jerk him
every time he offers any resistance. Now lead
him in front of the wagon; pull it towards him;
should he start, jerk him again, and so repeat
until you can pull the wagon up to him. Now
raise the shafts and let them down quietly over
his back; repeat this operation until he will remain perfectly quiet. Now lead him up, pulling
the wagon behind him. When he will bear this
nicely, you may hook him fast to the wagon, first
putting the long web upon the near front foot,

SAFE TO DRIVE.

pass it under the girth, and give it to an assistant; get into the wagon with your assistant, having previously instructed him how to manage the web. Have a second assistant to lead the animal a short distance; if he behaves well let him go. With this system, one-half hour's handling every day for a week is sufficient to break thoroughly to harness the wildest colt.

BITTING THE COLT.

The ordinary process of bitting colts is too well known to horsemen generally to need any description at my hands. A cheap and easy method of bitting colts, if properly managed, is by means of the cord. To arch the neck and bring the nose in where you want it, take the

cord using the small loop over the under jaw,
pass the cord over the neck from the off side, and
through the loop on the near side. Now take

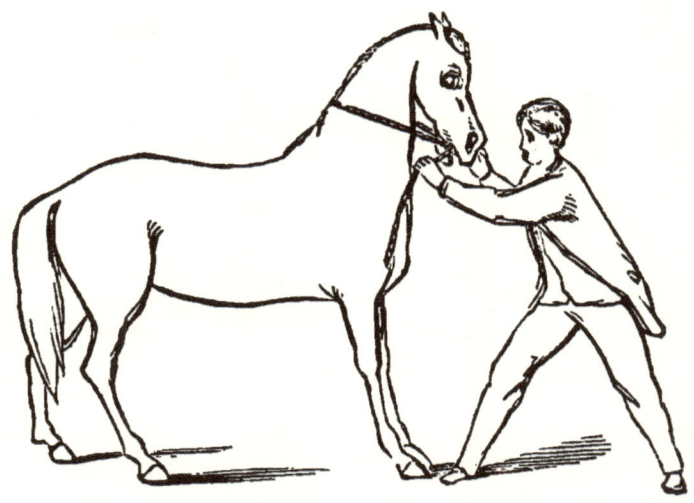

BITTING THE COLT.

your position at the near shoulder, press lightly
upon the cord; should the colt resist, let it loose
for a moment, then press upon it again, and as
he yields caress him; by repeating this a few
times, say two or three times a day as opportunity
offers, you will find he soon yields his head nicely.
Use the utmost care on first applying it, or you
will excite the colt to resistance. When once he
learns that he can resist successfully he will try
it over again. Do not continue the use of the
cord more than about ten minutes at a time.

Now change the end of the cord, taking the large loop, pass it over the neck, put the cord through the mouth from the off side, back through the loop on the near side, take your position in front of the animal, pull lightly upon the cord; this sets his head up as high as you want to put

SETTING UP THE HEAD.

it.   By repeating this lesson, the colt soon learns to get up his head on the slightest touch upon the rein.   The cord is also used,

TO ADD STYLE.

It will be observed in using the cord for the purpose of bitting the colt, that the small loop

7

brings the chin in towards the body, at the same
time beautifully arching the neck; the large loop
having directly the opposite effect by putting the
head up in any position desired. This arrangement applied to older horses, with a bad carriage
of the head, adds at least twenty per cent. to their
appearance, and often more than that amount to
their price.

MOUNTING THE COLT.

Take your position on the near side of the colt,
stand with your right side next to the animal,
take hold of the mane with your left hand, place
the toe of the left foot in the stirrup, placing the
right hand upon the back part of the saddle; now
raise yourself up with a quick spring, passing the
right leg over the saddle, and take your seat; a
very little practice will enable you to perform this
feat with ease and in a graceful manner. To
place your body fronting the side of the animal is
a very awkward position, and one rendering it
much more difficult to mount the animal. Should
the colt not stand well, a few jerks with the cord
will bring him to his senses, and make him stand
until you are seated. You are now prepared for

RIDING THE COLT.

In riding the colt for the first time, a common
riding bridle without martingale is to be preferred;
fasten the short web around the off fore foot, take
a short hold upon it with the right hand while

you sit upon his back, holding the bridle-rein in the left hand; should he act badly, pull up the off foot with the web, at the same time pat him gently upon the neck with the left hand; there is no danger in taking up the foot in this manner, provided you do not pull upon the reins at the same time. Let down the foot in a few minutes, and turn the colt around several times by pulling upon the off rein, then reverse the action by pulling upon the near rein; now turn him to the right, then to the left, several times. Should he still be restive, take up the foot again, and so repeat until he performs his part properly—then do not fail to caress him. Make the first lesson a short one, and gradually increase it from time to time as occasion may require. This method rarely requires the whip, and is certainly attended with less danger than the old and tedious one of riding a colt. We now come to

WHIP TRAINING.

To train a horse thoroughly to drive without bit or line under the whip, requires from four to six weeks' time; it requires also a man of strong nerve and self-control to be a successful trainer in this particular branch. Whip training illustrates the beauty and power of our system of horse training. Such a feat as driving a horse without bit or line cannot be accomplished by any other system known to man. Having selected a horse with a moderate share of intelligence, the next thing is to secure a suitable place for training. An inclosure twenty-five or thirty feet square is required. If you have it smaller, and your horse should be disposed to kick, you would be in danger; if larger, it gives the animal too much room to get away from the whip. It is better that you go in with the horse alone, as then the animal will have no other object to take his attention. Turn him loose without bridle or halter in the inclosure; take your position in the centre, holding in your right hand a straight whip nine or ten feet long; you crack the whip as you take your position; this alarms the horse and causes him to run into one corner of the inclosure; crack it several times that he may learn that you do not intend to hurt him; now commence tapping him lightly upon the near shoulder, but not to hurt him; if a nervy fellow he is all excitement for a few minutes; continue the tapping until he turns his head towards you, which he will do in a short time. The moment he turns it, however slight it may be, cease the whipping; as soon as he turns it away again repeat the tapping with the whip; in a few minutes he again turns his head towards you; stop the motion of the whip: as he turns away repeat the whip-tapping as before; in a very short time he turns around so that you can approach him; now gently caress him; move away and again approach him; should he turn away repeat the whipping: by this means you teach him to come to you on the near side. After he has learned this thoroughly, which re-

quires about one week's training, half an hour
each day, then proceed in the same manner upon
the off side; as soon as he obeys the motion of
the whip upon this side, take your position behind
him, and turn him by the motion of the whip, to
the right or to the left; as soon as he performs
nicely, put the harness upon him, take the lines
behind him, and, as you give him the word to
go forwards, throw the whip down by his right
side without touching him, at the same time
have the long web around the rear fore foot, and
give it to an assistant; you want him to stop,
give him the word *whoa*, at the same time your
assistant pulls up the foot, turn the whip in a
horizontal position above your head—in this way
you teach him that the whip in that position
means *whoa*. By repeating these motions, he
learns in about four weeks to turn to the right
whenever the whip is thrown towards the right
shoulder; to the left when thrown towards the
left shoulder; to go ahead when thrown down by
the right side; and to stop when held in a horizontal position. You now want to teach him to
back; having previously instructed him according to our rule, put the cord, using the small
loop, in his mouth; take the cord in your hand
with the reins, pull upon the reins, and say Back,
at the same time keep the whip directly over the
animal's back, giving it an upward and downward
motion, or you may tap him gently upon the back
with the whip—this is best done in a sulky. If
he starts forward, set him back by pulling quickly

7 *

upon the cord; repeat the operation until he will go back by the motion of the whip alone. Should he make repeated efforts to go forward, bring the whip quickly once or twice down over his nose, he will not then repeat the operation very often; with this training, it is necessary to use an open bridle, so that the animal will see the motions of the whip; you are now prepared to hook him up for the first drive. Take an assistant with you; have the foot-strap or long web secured upon the near fore foot; give it in charge of your assistant; let the lines lie over the dash, as a matter of precaution. Now commence operations with the whip; if the animal acts promptly, remove the foot web, and begin again, having the lines over the dash as before; drive the animal in this way at least two or three weeks before removing the bit from the mouth. Your horse is now safe to drive under the whip.

TO TEACH A HORSE TRICKS.

It is necessary, in teaching horses to perform tricks, to have in addition to the webbing the implements known as the Rarey straps, by which means you teach the animal to lie down, &c.

THE SHORT STRAP.

A common breeching strap is all that is necessary; it is used to strap up the foot (see engraving). Open the loop, keeping the buckle on the outside, put the loop over the foot, then raise the

THE SHORT STRAP.

foot and pass the strap around the fore-arm from
the inside, and buckle it tight; this holds the foot
up firmly.

PULLING UP THE FOOT.

THE LONG STRAP.

This is a strap which buckles around the foot. It has a ring in it, to which is buckled another strap seven or eight feet long, or the short web will answer the purpose. This is put upon the right foot passing it under the girth (see engraving at foot of p. 79), or over the back for the purpose of taking up the foot, when we want to bring the animal upon his knees.

TO TEACH A COLT TO FOLLOW YOU.

Take the cord, using the small loop, give him a few quick pulls right and left, then take your position on one side opposite the shoulder, give a quick pull upon the cord, which brings him towards you; at the same time say, Come here, sir; as he obeys, caress him. Repeat this until he will come without the pull, then take your position upon the other side and proceed in the same way. You will soon have him so that he will follow in any direction.

TO TEACH A HORSE TO LIE DOWN.

Take your position upon the near side; strap up the near fore foot, using the short strap; have a good strong bridle with cheek pieces, so, as to prevent the bit from pulling through the mouth. Tie a knot in the bridle-rein over the neck, take a short hold of the bridle-rein with the left hand, the right hand holding the off rein; now press him backwards, and as you do so he comes down

FOOT STRAPPED UP.

LEARNING TO LIE DOWN.

gently upon his near knee; let him rest awhile
in that position. Whenever he attempts to jump
pull him towards you, and press back as before;

THE STRUGGLE.

after repeating this two or three times most horses
will lie down; if you do not succeed, however,
put on the long strap, passing it under the girth,
or, what is better, over the back; take a short
hold of the strap with the right hand, pull him

PROPER POSITION.

towards you with the left hand, and as he steps
pull up the right foot, this brings him upon his

COMING ON HIS KNEES.

knees; keep him there until he lies down, then
caress him, handle him gently all over, knock his
feet together, pull his head up and lay it down

GETTING READY.

DOWN AT LAST.

carefully; repeat this operation several times, and he will soon learn to lie down by merely raising the near front foot, or lightly tapping it with a whip.

TO SIT UP.

Lay the animal down as previously directed, having a collar upon him; place a hobble or strap, with a ring in it, around each hind foot; take a pair of ordinary driving lines, pass the buckle-end through the collar back to the ring in the hobble, and buckle them; pull the feet up towards the shoulders, and carry the lines back to the hind quarters, hold them firmly in one hand, or give them to an assistant. Have a bridle with a long rein upon the animal; take the rein in your hand, stand upon the tail, and pull upon the bridle-rein, keeping the lines firm at the same time; this brings him up in front, and prevents his getting his hind feet back far enough to rise upon them, they being drawn forwards and securely held by the lines. Repeat the operation a few times—say two or three times a day—and he soon learns to lie down at the word. This is the method usually practised upon circus horses.

TO MAKE A HORSE BOW.

Stand upon the near side, and with a pin in your right hand prick the animal lightly in the breast, and say Make a bow, sir; he will soon learn to throw his head downwards; when he does so caress him; by repeating this operation a few

8

times he soon learns to bow by merely pointing the hand towards his breast, or if learned by a motion of the foot. In all cases when training horses to perform tricks, it is necessary that they should have a bridle without winkers, or else have the head bare.

TO ANSWER QUESTIONS.

Take your position as before, and with a pin in your right hand, prick him lightly anywhere along the mane or over the withers, (ask such questions as you want answered in the negative,) this causes him to shake his head, which he will do also when bothered with flies upon the neck during fly time. It was this circumstance which suggested the use of the pin to make a horse say no. By repeating this operation a few times he will shake his head by simply raising the hand to your head as if to raise your hat; this motion of the head indicates no. Nodding the head by pricking the breast signifies yes; always ask the question before making the motion with your hand.

TO KISS YOU.

To teach a horse to kiss you, take a piece of apple in your hand, let the horse smell it, he will then try to get it from you, carry it up to your mouth and hold it between your teeth, let him take it from your mouth; repeat this a few times and use the words, Kiss me; he soon learns that Kiss me, means apple, and he puts up his mouth to yours to take it away; when operating privately always give it to him, and he will then obey you promptly when showing him publicly.

TO SHAKE HANDS. .

Take your position in front of the horse, say Give me your right foot, or Shake hands; he does not understand you; you convey the idea to him by taking a pin and gently pricking him upon the right leg, he at once lifts it up; as he does so take it in your hand and caress him; he understands by this that he has done what you wanted him to do; after repeating this a few times, put your hand towards his leg and crack the thumb and fingers, he anticipating the prick lifts his foot; should he fail to do so have your pin handy and use it lightly. By this means he soon learns to give you the foot at the crack of the thumb and fingers. As soon as he gives one freely, teach him in the same manner to give the other one. .

TO KICK WITH THE RIGHT OR LEFT FOOT.

Care must be taken in teaching this trick, that you have a horse not predisposed to vicious propensities, or you may make a confirmed kicker; and then you will have the habit to break up. A horse of a mild disposition may be taught to perform thus without the risk of his becoming a kicker. I have taught one of my ponies to kick when I desire him to do so, and he cannot be made to kick unless the whip is used lightly upon his hind parts. Having selected your animal, take a pin in your right hand, prick the near hind leg with it and say Kick with the left foot; the animal soon learns to obey. Then proceed with the opposite leg in the same manner. After the horse will kick with either foot, by a motion of the hand without pricking him you will stand off a short distance, with a long whip in your hand; touch the near hind foot and say Kick with the left foot; then proceed in the same manner with the right foot. By proceeding thus once a day the animal will soon learn to do his part very nicely.

LEARNING TO WALTZ.

Some horses seem to love music, and can readily be taught to waltz or dance. Use a girth around the body, upon the near side of which buckle a short strap, having a loop at one end, to fasten to the ring of the bit; draw the strap through the girth buckle so as to incline the head a little to the near side; have one or two good pieces of music, and play any waltz that may be desired; at the same time turn the animal by the use of the whip lightly upon his legs; he soon learns to turn merely by a motion of the whip without touching him. After repeating this lesson once a day for three or four weeks, the strap may be removed, leaving his head free.

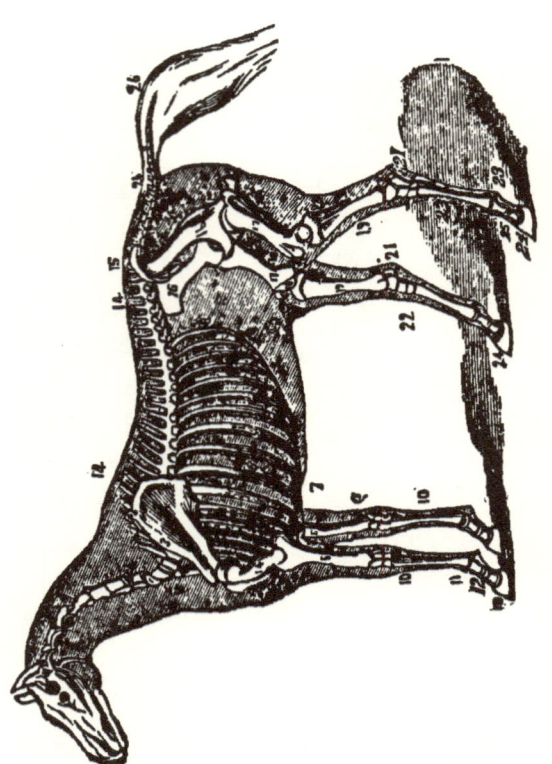

HINTS UPON SHOEING.

A glance at the skeleton of the horse will at once serve to convince us that the animal is formed at the same time for strength, and for celerity and ease of motion. If we look at the fore limbs we shall see that the scapula, No. 3, recedes ' from the shoulder-joint, falling back obliquely; its upper part uniting with the spinous processes of the anterior dorsal vertebræ, No. 14, to form the withers. The shoulder-bone No. 4 retreats, forming an angle at the elbow-joint; the fore arm consists of two pieces, No. 5, the radius and ulna consolidated as one bone in the mature horse; this is followed by a double row of small bones, No. 9, the carpus or wrist bones, seven in number. These are succeeded by the metacarpus, No. 10, with two slender splint bones attached posteriorly to its upper part. To these succeed the three phalangeal bones, Nos. 11, 12, and 13. There are besides a small pair of bones situated behind the fetlock joint called sessamoides, and a small bone situated behind, and between Nos. 12 and 13, called the navicular bone. The coffin bone, No. 13, is enclosed in the hoof, which consists of thick, firm, rounded horn, having a certain degree of expansibility; and underneath, forming a sort of sole, is a part called the frog; it is an elastic cushion, and in a healthy state prevents concussion. At each step the frog yields under the weight of the animal, and swelling out laterally expands the heels of the hoof. This frog ought always to touch the ground; it does so naturally, and where bad shoeing prevents it, the crust of the hoof soon becomes hard, brittle, and unyielding, causing a shock at every step as the animal trots over the hard road. Inflammation and alteration of structure soon supervene. The posterior limbs are modelled on a similar plan. Now from the angles which the bones of the limbs make with each other at the joints, the force of every shock as the animal trots or gallops is greatly broken; its very step is light and elastic; and this not only results from the obliquity of the bones in question, but particularly from the yielding spring of the pastern, its elasticity being provided for by a ligament which passes down the back of the cannon bone, No. 10, and along the pasterns to the coffin bone 11, 12, and 13. Nor is the spring of the elastic frog to be here overlooked; it also contributes an important share to the easy progression of the horse, the action of whose limbs as he moves is, or ought to be free, vigorous, and springy. But alas! how often do we see the knees distorted with overtoil, and the pasterns rigid and swollen from disease!

Shoeing is generally regarded as a necessary evil; and were it not for our paved streets and turnpiked roads, an evil which might in a great measure be well dispensed with. As it is, our object should be to observe as closely as possible three important rules in shoeing horses: 1st. To preserve the natural bearing of the foot: 2d. To preserve the hoof in its natural shape: 3d. To protect the foot from injury. If we observe the foot of the unshod horse, we find the hoof has a perfectly level bearing upon the crust or wall as it rests upon the ground, as well as upon the frog, which, as previously stated, acts as an elastic cushion preventing concussion and expanding the heels, which relieves the pressure upon the sensitive and delicate structure within the hoof, that otherwise would occur were the hoof hard and unyielding. It is unnecessary as well as uninteresting to the general reader for us to go into a minute description of the structure of the horse's foot. Those who desire such information can obtain it by consulting Jennings on "The Horse and his Diseases." The sole or ground surface of the foot is all that part of the foot situated between the frog and the crust or wall; this sole should not come in contact with either the ground or the shoe. Supposing now the reader to understand our meaning,

In order to preserve the level bearing of the foot, it is necessary that the shoe be made with a perfectly level surface upon the foot side, for the crust to rest upon. Beyond that point it should be bevelled inwards, in order to prevent pressure upon the sole. The frog should remain untouched with the knife, except to trim off any ragged edges. The moment the substance of the frog is cut away, that moment it begins to lose its moisture; hence its elasticity. It becomes hard and brittle often as the hoof itself; its function is thus destroyed, and it now acts as a foreign body, bruising the sole, causing diseases of various kinds to arise. If we examine the feet of horses shod in the ordinary manner—and there are few others—we find in place of the shoe having a level bearing for the crust, it is bevelled from without inwards, so that the foot rests upon a concave instead of a level surface. The consequence is, the heels, instead of expanding up these inclined planes, are actually pressed inwards, in consequence of the lateral pressure thus brought to bear upon them. This, as a natural result, causes contraction of the hoof sooner or later, causing a hard, brittle condition of the hoof, predisposing it to split, producing toe, quarter, or other cracks, which never occur in an elastic hoof; corns soon follow contraction of the hoof, often producing very severe lameness, and leading to diseases of a more serious nature. When we have a contracted foot, it is only necessary to reverse the bearing of the shoe —that is, the bearing at the heels back from the last nail-hole should be very slightly bevelled outwards. This has a direct tendency to gradually facilitate the expansion of the heels. Dr. R. Jennings's Hoof Ointment is one of the best applications that can be made to a contracted hoof; it restores its elasticity, and promotes a healthy condition of the hoof. And here let me caution the smith, in bevelling the shoe, to give it a very little slant, from the last nail-hole on either side,

not more than the twentieth part of an inch;
otherwise more harm than good will be likely to
follow its application.

PREPARING THE FOOT FOR THE SHOE.

This, as a mechanical operation, requires a man
if good, sound judgment to properly perform his
work.   The growth of the hoof is about equal to
its wear when the animal remains unshod, otherwise the hoof would be worn too short or become
too long.   Our object, then, in paring the foot,
is to remove so much of the hoof as would have
been worn away had not the shoe prevented such
wear.   Any deviation from this rule causes the
feet to become unusually long, the sole thick, &c.,
causing the animal to stumble at almost every
step.   In preparing the foot for the shoe, after
carefully removing any old stubs that might remain, the crust should be lowered with the rasp
from the toe to the heels, the sole then should
be pared with the drawing-knife in preference to
the buttress.   The feet should be poulticed the
night before being shod, with linseed meal; this
will so soften the hoof as to enable the smith to
pare the feet without difficulty.   Care must be
taken to remove a portion of the horn between
the crust and bars, so that the heels of the crust
should be higher than the heels of the sole.   The
bars will simply require cleaning out, removing
any loose portions without diminishing their
strength.   All ragged portions of the frog should
be removed, but the frog must by no means be

cut away merely because the smith fancies it to be too large. In weak feet, very little paring is required; the heels, however, require the nicest care for their protection from injury in shoeing. No fixed rules can be laid down for paring the feet; that must be determined by the nature and condition of these appendages.

APPLICATION OF THE SHOE TO THE FOOT.

The shoe should be set as near the outer margin of the crust as possible; by so doing, we have the crust as the main support of the foot, as nature intended it should be. By setting the shoe back a quarter or three-eighths of an inch from the outer margin of the crust, as is often done, at least one-half of the bearing surface of the foot is destroyed. It is therefore weakened in exact proportion as it is cut away, besides greatly reducing the space for driving the nails, thus rendering them more liable to do injury, by being driven too close to the sensitive structure, or by pricking the foot. The nails should be pointed with great care, in order that they may be driven with a greater degree of certainty. Eight nail-holes are usually punched in the shoe; but our experience teaches us that injury is often prevented by leaving out the quarter nail upon the inside of the foot. If it should be thought necessary, it may be put in at the toe instead.

CLIPS UPON THE SHOE.

These should not be used, as they are the*
frequent cause of an obscure lameness, often
giving rise to much trouble. The growth of the
horn being from above downwards, the clip offers
an obstruction to the growth of the hoof, which
cannot be overcome; hence it is turned inwards
upon the soft structures of the foot. This is
readily seen after death, in the hoof of a horse
which has been shod several years with the clip.
Removal of the cause will enable the animal to
get entirely over the lameness in two or three
months. I have restored horses to perfect soundness in this way very frequently, even after a
lameness of two and three years' standing. When
it is thought necessary to use a clip, one of the
smallest kind should be employed.

INTERFERING.

Many horses are in the habit of interfering
and many ingenious methods have from time to
time been devised to prevent this troublesome
habit. Both the hind and fore legs are subject
to cutting or striking, usually about the fetlock
joint. In the front feet, however, we sometimes
find them striking just below the knee-joint,
producing an enlargement known as a speedy
cut. We should, when this habit exists, first
ascertain the cause as nearly as possible, and the
part which strikes, whether the shoe or the foot.
Many horses interfere only when leg-weary. Par-
9

ticularly is this the case with colts. Some horses strike when shod with heavy shoes, but do not do so with light ones. Others interfere from some peculiarity in the conformation of the limbs. The most successful plan of preventing this habit, is to ·straighten the inside of the shoe from the toe to the quarter, allowing the heel of the shoe on the inside the same inclination that it .would have ordinarily applied. Two nails only should be driven on the inside of the foot with this shoe. This is an exception to our rule in applying the shoe, but it usually has the desired effect. By no means make the shoe higher on one side than the other, as it causes unequal concussion upon the limb when the animal is in motion; hence predisposing the joints to injury. In some rare cases, widening the web of the shoe, as well as straightening it upon the inside, has the desired effect, when simply straightening fails to accomplish the purpose.

OVERREACHING.

Many very good horses have this troublesome habit. Young horses are more subject to over-reaching than old ones; it very frequently disappears as the speed of the animal is increased. At a moderate gait the front feet do not always get out of the way in time for the hind ones as they are brought forwards, hence a collision takes place. ·Sometimes the heels are cut or bruised badly, and occasionally the shoes are torn from the front feet. The most successful means of preventing this habit, is to make the front shoes a little lighter, which facilitates their motion, the animal lifting them up so quickly—the hind ones should be a little heavier. Trifling as this difference may appear, it is very generally successful; an ounce of iron will make a very marked difference in the movement of most animals, as much so as weight upon the back.

SHOEING HORSES WITH CORNS.

The corn should be well cut out, and then burned with a red-hot iron, muriatic acid, or butter of antimony. The shoe recommended for contracted feet should be here applied; the hoof backwards from the corn to the heel should be removed, so that no part of the hoof back from the corn have any bearing upon the shoe; by this means we prevent all concussion that otherwise would fall upon the part affected; the animal thus shod will travel sound though the corn be a bad one. Much depends upon the careful and skilful application of the shoe, independently of its being constructed on proper principles. Many horses with very bad feet are enabled to go sound for years by a combination of care and skill, while on the contrary a single shoeing done by a bungling workman would suffice to lame them. It requires considerable skill to fit a shoe properly on a bad foot, so as to save the weakest parts and economize the horn.

STOPPING THE FEET.

When we take into consideration the unnatural condition in which the feet of the horse in a state of domestication are brought, by nailing upon them the iron shoe, and standing them upon plank floors, we can readily understand why it is, that the hoof so soon becomes hard, brittle, and contracted. 1st. There is no moisture absorbed by the foot from either the shoe or the plank. If we stand the horse upon the ground, it is but little better, as such floors are usually very dry, or else they are in a filthy condition in consequence of the urine which the animal has passed off, predisposing the feet to thrush, &c. In consideration of the above facts it is our duty to protect the feet by artificial means. To do this effectually, the feet should be stopped with flaxseed meal mixed with water, that is when the meal is mixed the soles should be packed full, say once or twice a week during the winter season, and three or four times a week during the summer season. A small quantity of Dr. R. Jennings's Hoof Ointment applied to the upper part of the crust will be found of very great advantage; it softens the hoof and causes a healthy secretion of horn, or hoof. For a more perfect description of shoeing and the injuries consequent thereto, see Dr. R. Jennings on " The Horse and his Diseases."

THINGS WORTH KNOWING.

A man to control a horse must learn to control

himself. What you do must be done thoroughly, or better not do it at all.

Once handling a horse produces but a tempopary effect. "A merciful man is merciful to his beast."

On first hitching a colt in the stable, put a rope behind him, so that he cannot pull back upon the halter. Light stables are preferable to dark ones. Why? On taking a horse from a dark stable the pupil of the eye is dilated, in consequence of the change from a dark place to a light one; the pupil is acted upon too suddenly and severely; the result is, the animal cannot distinguish objects until the pupil of the eye contracts.

Stuff the feet often, and use occasionally Dr. R. Jennings's Hoof Ointment, if you would keep the feet of your horses in a healthy condition.

Drive fast, and stop often.

Pay the groom liberally, it will pay you back in the care of your horse.

To warrant a horse free from vice is to make use of an almost indefinite term, for its boundaries are neither well defined nor understood; and under this sweeping term might be included many faults generally considered trivial. Slipping the collar, weaving in the stall, &c., might all equally be construed into vice.

To warrant a horse perfectly free from vice is great folly, because it will always admit of a quibble.

In law, the word "warranted" extends merely

9*

to soundness; "warranted sound" has no greater extent.

"Warranted sound, free from vice, and quiet to ride or drive," covers everything but age. The warranty should always be written. If you are about purchasing a horse, it would be to your interest to cousult some reliable veterinary surgeon. Things which cost least are not always the cheapest, but prove in the end very dear. Cheapness is the surest bait in the world.

Quantity may be estimated by an uneducated eye: to discern the quality of anything, requires experience and judgment. If you have a horse you wish to match, do not let the dealer know your object, or he will demand a higher price.

"The eye of the master makes the horse fat."

"He who buys, had need have an hundred eyes."

"What is everybody's business is nobody's business."

Try before you buy.

To make a horse have a fine coat,

Feed well, clothe warmly, sweat often, groom well, and use Dr. R. Jennings's Condition Powder.

To remove a horse from a burning stable, blindfold him.

Never quarrel with your horse.

Wet the hay for a horse with heaves, and use Dr. R. Jennings's Heave or Cough Powder.

Good grooming promotes the health of horses.

Never let your horse know that he can resist you.

Never bleed a horse when the membrane lining the nose presents a bluish appearance, as it denotes a debilitated condition of the system; under such circumstances the animal wants a liberal diet, and strong tonic treatment.

Never drench a horse if it can be avoided, but always administer medicine in the form of ball or powder. The anatomical structure of the horse's throat renders drenching exceedingly dangerous.

Drenching is the best way of administering medicine to cattle.

To ball a horse properly, take the tongue in the left hand, bringing it out on the off-side of the mouth, then take the ball in the right hand between the thumb and first two fingers, pass it over the curve of the tongue, and let it go; do not be in too much of a hurry, or you will be likely to fail in giving it.

Never feed corn or corn meal to horses which are not in a healthy condition.

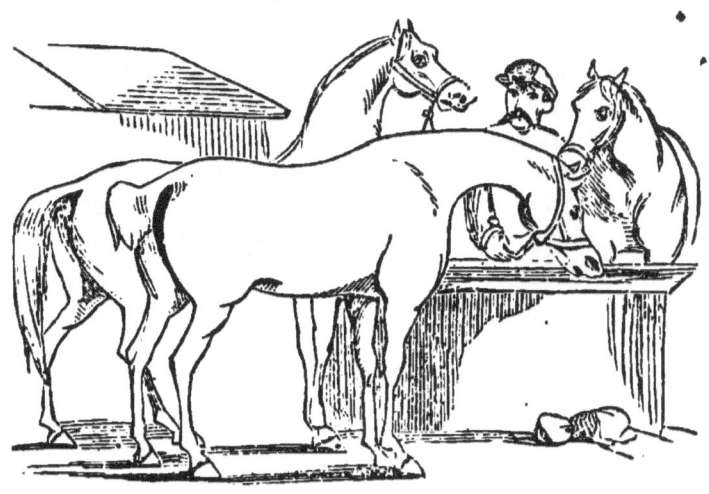

DISEASES OF THE HORSE.

This noble animal, more than any other of our domestic animals, is subject to diseases, which are as numerous and varied as are those of man, generally assuming an inflammatory character of either the sthenic or asthenic form. By

STHENIC INFLAMMATION

We mean its acute form, which is the most common stage of inflammation. It is generally rapid in its attacks, certain in its cause, quick in its course, or in the development of its terminations or consequences, and strongly marked in its symptoms and attendant fever. The most acute forms of inflammation are Founder, Inflammation of the Bowels, Lymphatics, Lungs, and other forms of chest and abdominal inflammations.

ASTHENIC INFLAMMATION.

This is characterized by a feeble and debilitated state of the organism; by an uncertainty in many instances as to the real nature of its cause; by an insidiousness in its progress; by a want of that precise certainty in its symptoms, which is so characteristic a feature of the acute sthenic kinds; by being attended with fever of a low typhoid nature; and, by its greater proneness in the generality of cases to spread to nearly all the soft tissues, and terminate in gangrene and death. The most common forms in which asthenic inflammation is manifested are those of Typhoid, Pleuro-Pneumonia, the ordinary Typhoid Influenza, Scarlatina Maligna, &c.

TERMINATIONS OF INFLAMMATION.

Inflammation has several terminations, which are designated by the following terms:—Resolution, Mortification, Suppuration, Ulceration, Hemorrhage, Effusion, Hepatization, and Ossification.

By *Resolution*, is meant, comparative restoration to health.

Mortification, death of the parts involved.

Suppuration, a breaking up of tissues, and formation of purulent matter, which receives the name of abscess.

Ulceration, the formation of an ulcer; a purulent solution of continuity of the soft parts.

Hemorrhage occurs from rupture of blood-vessels, wounds, ulcers penetrating the coats of an artery, &c.

Effusion, watery accumulations; a serous fluid as in dropsy.

Hepatization, liver-like structures changed in their character, assuming the appearance of liver.

Ossification, change of soft structures into bony ones.

Adhesion, two or more separate structures becoming united. We briefly allude to the subject of inflammation in order to give the general reader some landmarks by which to form tolerably correct conclusions regarding the character of such diseases as they may chance to meet with.

DISEASES OF THE MOUTH.

LAMPAS.

Lampas, as it is termed, is a fullness or swelling of the gums and the bars or roof of the mouth, consequent upon cutting the teeth. Lampas is usually found in all colts during the period of dentition. Many, however, suffer little or no inconvenience by them, while in others the great tenderness of the gums and bars causes the animal to refuse his food. The owner too often, with a vague idea of relief, submits the animal to the cruel operation of burning out the bars with a red-hot iron. A very few years since, and I may add still is, in many sections of the country, almost the only course pursued in such cases, notwithstanding it is of no practical benefit whatever; but on the contrary is often very injurious. The only treatment required, is to lance the parts freely, and wash the mouth with a solution of tincture of myrrh, one ounce to three of water; give no hay or corn for a week.

BAGS, OR WASHERS.

The bit, in reining, frequently bruises the lining membrane of the mouth, causing soft puffy swellings within the corners of the lips; these sometimes become so large as to cause much inconvenience to the animal in masticating his food. For their removal the part should be freely lanced and allowed to bleed undisturbed; then bathe the parts with the following wash :—

> R. Tincture of Myrrh.
> Tincture of Aloes.
> Rain-water, equal parts.

Mix all together.

Should this not succeed, remove the swellings with the knife, or what is as well, clip them off with a pair of scissors, then apply the above wash to the wound two or three times a day, until healed.

SORE MOUTH.

This is caused also by the bearing of the bit. upon tender-mouthed horses. It is situated at the corners of the mouth, often causing considerable thickening of the lips about the parts affected. Alum-water should be applied to the parts three times a day, or the wash for bags, or washers, may be used with equal advantage.

ULCERS IN THE MOUTH.

In breaking horses to harness, the under jaw, immediately in front of the molar teeth, is sometimes so injured by the bit as to cause inflammation of the periosteum (a thin membrane which covers the bone), occasionally causing caries of the bone, in consequence of which pipe-like openings called sinuses are formed, which, becoming filled with partly-masticated food, soon becomes fetid, and often occasions sores which prove troublesome to heal. When the gum only is injured, it should be carefully washed with tincture of myrrh and water, equal parts; but when the bone is involved, the diseased parts must be removed, and afterwards dressed with the following lotion :—

R. Gallic Acid,	1 ounce.
Tincture of Opium,	1 "
Water,	4 "

Mix all together, and bathe the parts affected two or three times a day.

WOLF TEETH.

Many horsemen regard these teeth as injurious to the eyes of horses; but we cannot understand upon what principle their opinions are based. These teeth are not supernumary teeth as has been asserted by many writers, but on the contrary are natural to all horses. The germs or pulps of these teeth are in the jaw at the time of foaling, and are developed generally at one year old, ready to cut their way through the gums. All young animals of the equine species have these teeth, and they can be found in the mouths of four out of five colts at two years of age. It is only when the eyes are affected by disease that these teeth are looked for, and when found are supposed by some to be the cause of the trouble. In an experience of twenty years, I have not been able to discover the least connection between these teeth and the eyes. And what is equally singular, these teeth are seldom mentioned by veterinary

authors. If you find them in your colts, and
wish them removed, the best plan is to pull them
out with a pair of ordinary tooth forceps. See
Jennings on "The Horse and his Diseases."

IRREGULAR TEETH

In old horses the molar teeth, or grinders, frequently become very uneven upon their grinding
surfaces, causing difficulty in masticating the
food ; the outer edges of the upper molars becoming sharp cut the cheeks, causing them to become
sore, and often very much swollen. The remedy
is the tooth rasp, by which the sharp edges of the
teeth are taken off, enabling the animal to again
masticate his food in a proper manner.

CARIES OF THE TEETH.

Horses frequently suffer from this troublesome
disease. Caries or decay in the teeth gives rise
to the tooth-ache the same as in man, causing
symptoms in the horse which are often mistaken
for other affections. My work on the horse ex-
plains this subject more fully. When caries has
existed for some time, there will be as a general
thing a fetid discharge from one nostril; the food
passes away in an undigested state, particularly
is this the case when whole corn has been given;
loss of flesh, stupor, starring coat, stopping short
in the road when in harness, shaking the head
and then going on again, starting as though
scared when no objects of fear are about. The

10

only remedy is the removal of the teeth, which generally requires the aid of a qualified veterinary surgeon.

DISEASES OF THE EYE.

AMAUROSIS OR GLASS EYE.

In this disease we observe a clear bright eye, well calculated to deceive the best horsemen, and it is not until the animal runs against some object in his way that blindness is suspected. It is a very easy matter, however, to detect the amaurotic eye. The pupil is always larger than usual, and on removing the animal from a strong to a weak light, and *vice versa*, no change is observed in the pupil, the light not having any effect upon it, which is not the case in the eye of a horse having his sight perfect. It is caused by paralysis of the optic nerve. Treatment.—This is uncertain, but occasionally the following is successful :—

R. Barbadoes aloes	6 drs.
Pulverized Ginger,	1 "
" Gentian,	1 "
Nitrate of Potassa,	1 "

Mix with molasses in the form of a ball and give to the horse. In twenty-four hours after giving the ball, give half drachm doses of pulverized nux vomica mixed in the feed night and morning; and apply a blister under the ears.

INFLAMMATION OF THE HAW.

This is an inflammation of the membrana nicti-tans situated at the inner corner of the eye, the function of which is to cleanse the eye of any dirt or other foreign substance which may get into it; when inflamed it becomes timid, causing a bulging at the inner corner of the eye, and is commonly known by the term hooks, or haw, in the eye. The treatment consists in bathing the eye with the following wash, two or three times a day:—

R.	Tincture Opium,	½ ounce.
	Tincture Aconite,	2 drachms.
	Rainwater,	1 pint.

Mix all together. Give a purgative ball, but do not under any circumstances have them cut out, as you thus deprive the animal of the means of cleansing the eye of dirt, or other matter getting into this delicate organ.

SIMPLE OPHTHALMIA.

This is simply an inflammation of the eye, caused generally by blows, or some other external injury. Bathe the eye with cold water, and give the following ball :—

R.	Barbadoes aloes,	1 ounce.
	Ginger pulverized,	1 drachm.
	Gentian "	½ "

Mix with water.

Bleeding under the eye is sometimes an advantage.

SPECIFIC OPHTHALMIA.

This is commonly known as moon blindness; the attack is sudden, the eye becomes watery and exceedingly tender, the lining of the eyelid is very red, and the eye itself is cloudy or white in appearance. The treatment consists in opening the bowels well with the purgative ball recommended in Amaurosis, and to bathe the eye with the following wash.

R. Tincture of Opium,   1 ounce.
Rainwater.   1 pint.

Mix both together.

This disease being of a specific character, its termination is sooner or later confirmed blindness; though the animal may have a number of attacks previous to its final termination.

CATARACT.

This is one of the terminations of specific ophthalmia. It is a breaking up of the crystalline lens of the eye, situated immediately behind the pupil. When diseased it presents one or more white spots, which gradually blend together until the whole lens is involved. There is no cure: operations only partially restore the sight, causing the animal to become a shyer, which is certainly more dangerous than blindness..

DISTEMPER.

This term is used by horsemen to denote all classes of catarrhal affections. A common cold,

influenza, bronchitis, &c., are all included under
the above heading. We are not disposed, however,
to regard the term distemper on so broad a field,
and will therefore drop it from our nomenclature
altogether; and consider the various diseases
under their proper headings.

SORE THROAT.

This is usually an accompanyment of catarrhal
affections. It sometimes occurs independently of
any such diseases; it is then known as laryngitis.
Symptoms.—Stiffness of the neck, cough, difficulty in swallowing, mouth full of saliva, with
more or less fever. Treatment,—apply the following liniment to the throat externally :—

R. Linseed oil,	3 ounces.
Cantharides ointment,	1 ounce.
Spirits of Turpentine,	1 "

Mix all together.
Or what is a better application, Dr. R. Jennings's
Sweating Liniment. It may be obtained of
Druggists and dealers generally; and give internally Dr. R. Jennings's Tonic Powder, it seldom
requires more than one box to effect a perfect
cure.

STRANGLES.

This is a more aggravated form of sore throat,
attended with considerable swelling of the throat
externally, often threatening suffocation. In very
bad cases the aid of a veterinary surgeon should
10 *

be had if possible; in the absence of such assistance, poultice the throat with linseed meal; pour scalding water upon some wheat bran and steam the nostrils with it, put a bag over the nose to prevent the steam from escaping too much; when the swelling becomes soft lance it under the jaw; the danger generally is past when it discharges freely. Give internally Dr. R. Jennings's Tonic Powder.

INFLUENZA.

This disease is supposed to result from some miasma in the atmosphere. It occurs in the spring and fall months, at times assuming a very malignant form, at other times it is comparatively mild in its attacks.

Symptoms.—A thin mucus discharge from the nostrils. The living membrane of the eyelids present an orange red appearance. The corners of the eyes are filled at times with a purulent matter; the animal is very much debilitated, as may be observed by its motion in the walk; the membrane of the nose is also reddened; cough attended with sore throat. In this disease metastic inflammation frequently occurs; by metastic we mean a change in the seat of disease in this case from the air passages to the feet, producing symptoms very similar to founder, which often is mistaken for that disease. A sustaining treatment is here required. In the early stages of the disease, give ten drops of Flemming's tincture of aconite in a little water upon the tongue every six hours, until the fever is checked; then give Dr. R. Jennings's Tonic Powder, it being prepared expressly for this class of disease. When the throat is sore use Dr. R. Jennings's Sweating Liniment.

BRONCHITIS.

This is an inflammation of the air-tubes (bronchial) of the lungs, usually accompanied with a painful cough, sore throat, mouth full of saliva, discharge from the nose, respiration disturbed, pulse quick, lining membrane of the nose and eyelids reddened. On applying the ear to the sides, a bubbling sound is heard, like the agitation of a fluid.

Treatment.—Give the following ball, and if the fever is not broken in twelve hours, repeat:—

> R. Pulv. Saltpetre,   2 drachms.
> " Digitalis
> Emetic Tartar, of each, ½ drachm.

Mix with honey or molasses; or, use

> R. Nitrate of Potash,   1½ oz.
> " Soda,   6 oz.

Mix, and divide into six doses. Give one three times a day in a sloppy mash. Apply to the throat Dr. R. Jennings's Sweating Liniment; and, when convalescent, Dr. R. Jennings's Tonic Powder may be used with great advantage in restoring strength and vigor to the system.

NASAL GLEET.

This is usually the result of neglected catarrh. It is attended with a chronic discharge from one

or both nostrils of a thin, whitish mucus.   The
animal's health is usually good, feeding and work-
ing as in perfect health.   The only treatment
which has proved successful is a sustaining one.
Give the following powders night and morning
in the feed :—

R. Sesquichloride of Iron,	2 oz.
Powdered Cinnamon,	1 "
" Gentian Root,	1 "
" Quassia, .	1 "

Mix all together, and divide into eight powders; or, use the following powders night and
morning in the feed:—

R. Muriate of Barytes,	1 oz.
Linseed Farina,	2 "

Mix, and divide into sixteen powders.

PLEURISY.

Inflammation of the lining membrane of the
chest and investing membrane of the lungs, is
know as pleuritis, or pleurisy, which requires
prompt treatment, or it is apt to terminate in
dropsy of the chest. *Symptoms.*—Pain on pressing the sides, a grunt peculiar to this disease,
pawing, the animal looking or biting at his sides,
pulse quick, temperature of the body much above
the natural heat, lying down but rising quickly.
Treatment.—Give ten drops of tincture of aconite
root, in a little water, every three hours for the
first two days : give in every pail of water one
ounce of nitric ether, and use Dr. R. Jennings's

Sweating Liniment on the sides; keep the body warm, and give no corn or corn meal.

INFLAMMATION OF THE LUNGS.

This disease occurs in the spring and fall, and is known to horsemen as lung fever. *Symptoms.* —Pulse quick and thready, mouth hot, the animal hangs his head in or under the manger, legs and ears cold, appetite lost, respiration quickened; on applying the ear to the side a crackling sound is heard. This disease requires prompt treatment, as it frequently terminates fatally in a few hours. If the animal is in a plethoric condition, bleeding is attended with beneficial results. Give five drops of tincture of aconite root, in a little water, upon the tongue every two hours, until the respiration becomes more tranquil; apply Dr. R. Jennings's Sweating Liniment to the sides. Injections of castile soap and water are very useful; or, what is better, injections of tobacco-smoke. The legs should be well hand-rubbed, and stimulated with mustard or cayenne pepper, and then wrapped in flannel bandages.

CONGESTIVE PNEUMONIA.

This disease is caused by some impure condition of the atmosphere, violent exercise, or sudden changes in the temperature of the air, &c. The blood ceases to circulate through the lungs, remaining there in a congested state; the pulse is full, but its action cannot be detected. Speedy resort to the lancet is our only hope here. Bleed freely and quickly, then place the animal in a box-stall, where the atmosphere is pure, and give the following twice a day :—

> R. Tincture of Opium,　　　2 drachms.
> Liquor Ammonia Acetatis, 2 oz.

Mix both together, and add one gill of water. Place a pail of bran slop before the animal, and keep the body warm; stimulate the legs, as in inflammation of the lungs, and wrap them in flannel bandages.

HYDROTHORAX.

Dropsy of the chest, is usually the termination of pleurisy. *Symptoms.*—Pulse small and quick, respiration quick and short, legs set wide apart, breast, belly, and sheath swollen; the animal never lies down. There is much prostration of strength in this disease, making the chances of recovery very doubtful. The treatment which has proved the most successful, is setons in the breast, and half-drachm doses of the iodide of potassa in water three times a day.

HEAVES, OR BROKEN WIND.

This disease is so well known that it does not require any special remark. When seated in the lungs, it is out of the reach of medicine, except as palliatives. The best preparation for this disease is Dr. R. Jennings's Cough or Heave Powder; or, use the following :—

> R. Assafœtida,　　2 drachms.
> Gum Camphor, 1 drachm.

Mix, and give every other night for a week. The hay should be well sprinkled with water; avoiding clover hay or corn.

PALPITATION OF THE HEART.

This disease is known to horsemen as the thumps. It is an inflammation of the lining membrane of the heart. *Symptoms.* — Heart pulsates violently, and may be observed at some distance from the animal; pulse full and hard. This disease is regarded as incurable. We can, however, palliate the worst cases in one or two hours' time, so that the animal is ready for work the following day. Divide one drachm of pulverized digitalis leaves into five powders; give one powder every fifteen minutes; keep the body warm, and give food sparingly for a day or two.

INFLAMMATION OF THE BRAIN.

This disease is known as mad staggers. It arises from blows over the head, over-feeding, particularly with corn ; a tight collar will sometimes produce it, &c. *Symptoms.*—Disinclination to move about, lining membrane of the eyelids much reddened, appetite lost, eyes present a dull, sleepy appearance; to these succeed delirium or madness. The animal now becomes indifferent to all about him, plunges about, destroying everything in his way that will yield to his struggles. *Treatment.*—Bleed freely, before the mad stage comes on, or you must wait until the animal falls

from exhaustion, then put the lancet into the
jugular vein, bleed almost to fainting; apply
bags of broken ice to the head, and open the
bowels with the following ball :—

        R. Barb. Aloes,   1 oz.
           Croton Oil,   6 drops.
           Pulv. Ginger,   1 drachm.

Mix with water, molasses, or honey.

Injections are also very beneficial. Give no
food of any kind for twenty-four hours. Corn
should not be given to animals subject to such
attacks of disease.

STOMACH STAGGERS.

This is the result of an overloaded stomach,
pressing upon the heart and lungs. The animal
appears dull and stupid, with a tendency to pitch
forwards unless supported by a wall, manger, tree,
or other object; constipation of the bowels usually
accompanies this disease. *Treatment.*—Bleed
freely, and open the bowels with the ball recommended for inflammation of the brain. Give no
food for forty-eight hours after the attack.

INFLAMMATION OF THE BOWELS.

Enteritis, or inflammation of the bowels, sometimes makes its appearance very insidiously; at
other times it is sudden in its attack. *Symptoms.*—Pulse full, strong, and quick, pawing, lying down, rolling on the back, kicking the belly,
body hot, legs cold, no intermissions of pain, as

in colic. *Treatment.*—Copious bleeding is very necessary in this disease; give five drops of Flemmings's Tincture of Aconite in a little water every two hours; blankets saturated with water as hot as the animal can bear them should be strapped around the body, and kept wet with hot water for two or three hours ; then remove, and replace them with dry ones. Tobacco-smoke injections are here very serviceable, or castile soap and water will answer a very good purpose. Give no food for forty-eight hours.

COLIC.

This disease occurs in two forms, flatulent and spasmodic colic. In the former there is considerable swelling of the abdomen, the animal throws itself about as in inflammation of the bowels; the pulse, however, is nearly in a natural condition, and there are intermissions from pain. In spasmodic colic, the same symptoms are present, with the exception of swelling of the abdomen. *Treatment.*—Give one-third of a bottle of Kerr's East India Liniment, prepared by Jennings & Higgins. This is the best preparation that can be used; or, give the following :—

> R. Tincture of Opium,   1 oz.
> Sulphuric Ether,   ½ "
> Water,   ½ pint.

Mix all together, and drench. If not relieved in half an hour, repeat the dose; rub the belly well with mustard and vinegar.

11

DIARRHŒA.

This disease is sometimes caused by the too free use of cathartic medicines, change of water, exposure to cold, &c. *Treatment.*—Give of Kerr's East India Liniment 3 oz. in one pint of water. The advantage of this Liniment is, it does not constipate the bowels; yet it has the desired effect by restoring healthy action in the digestive organs; or, give the following :—

R. Pulv. Opium,	1 scruple.
" Gentian Root,	1 drachm.
" Ginger "	1 "

Mix all together, and give every six hours until relieved; or, use the following :—

R. Gum Camphor, pulv.,	2 drachms.
Rhubarb, "	3 "
Opium, "	1 "

Mix all together, and give in half a pint of warm ale.

WORMS.

All animals are subject to these parasites; and thousands of animals are annually lost, without the cause being suspected. *Symptoms.*—Starring coat, haggard eye, colicky pains, gasping, debility, sluggish movements, emaciation, skin covered with scurfy blotches, small feeble pulse, belly tucked up, respiration slow, a peculiar pallid appearance of the membrane lining the mouth, irregular appetite, badly-digested fæces, agitation of the heart and tail, dung covered with a mucous

substance, a whitish or yellowish white substance about the fundament, rubbing the tail, &c.
These symptoms do not all appear in the same
animal. *Treatment.*—Use Dr. R. Jennings's
Worm Powder, the best preparation known for
worms; or, use the following, which in some
cases will answer the purpose :—

R. Oil of Male Ferns,	1 oz.	
Powd. Ginger,	¼	"
" Linseed,	½	"

Mix with molasses for one ball, repeat the dose
once a day for a week, then give an active purge;
or, the following will in some cases be found very
useful :—

R. Assafœtida,	2 drachms.	
Oil of Male Ferns,	½	"
Calomel,	1	"
Savin,	1	"
Linseed Meal,	2	"

Mix with molasses, and form a ball; give at
night, and follow it the next morning by giving
a purgative ball.

RETENTION OF URINE.

This is caused by irritation of the neck of the
bladder, or a dislike to spatter the legs. *Symptoms.*
—Frequent efforts to stale. Shake up the litter
under him, and he will urinate freely, unless the
retention is the result of disease, when such
means will fail. An instrument made for the
purpose, called a catheter, should be passed up
the urinary passage, first having it well greased

with lard; the urine will then flow freely, and give instant relief. If there is any fever present, give the following :—

R. Nitrate Potassa,   1 oz.
   Pulv. Digitalis,   1 drachm.
   Calomel,   1   "

Mix all together, and divide into eight powders; give one on the tongue three times a day; or,

R. Sulphate of Iron,   1 oz.
   Nit. Potassa,   1   "
   Rosin,   ½   "
   Juniper Berries, pulv. 2 "

Mix; and divide into four powders; give one night and morning. Injections of castile soap and water are very useful; or, where it can be resorted to, tobacco-smoke is preferable.

PROFUSE STALING.

This disease arises from the too free use of diuretic medicines, mow-burnt or musty hay, &c. Some persons are constantly giving their horses resin, saltpetre, and other diuretic drugs, which have a tendency to produce diseases of the urinary organs. This disease, as a general thing, is easily remedied; give the following :—

R. Prepared Chalk,   1 oz.
   Pulv. Opium,   2 drachms.
   "   Catechu,   ½ oz.

Mix, and divide into six powders, one to be given in the feed three times a day, until the desired effect is obtained; then give Dr. R. Jennings's Condition Powder.

BLOODY URINE.

Hematura, or bloody urine, is caused by strain of the loins, calculous concretions in the kidneys or ureters, unwholesome food, rupture of small blood-vessels about the bladder, &c. *Treatment.* —Give flaxseed-tea to drink, and open the bowels with a strong purgative ball, and give twice a day Dr. R. Jennings's Condition Powder.

CALCULI; OR, STONE IN THE BLADDER.

A horse may have these deposits in the bladder a long time before they occasion any very serious disturbance in the system. *Symptoms.*— Frequent efforts to stale, but voiding the urine in very small quantities at a time, which usually is of a turgid yellow or thick whitish color; colicky pains are often observed, the animal kicks its belly, paws, looks at its sides, and on changing its position frequently gets relief. *Treatment.*— Give twice a day one drachm of muriatic acid in a pail of water. Should this fail to give relief, an operation for the removal of the stone should be resorted to; this will require the assistance of a competent veterinary surgeon. (See Dr. Jennings on "The Horse and his Diseases.") I have operated on some nine or ten horses for this disease, and with entire success in every instance.

11*

HIDE-BOUND.

This is often caused by some slight disturbance in the system (occasionally from the action of worms), without producing any marked symptoms of disease. In all such cases, Dr. R. Jennings's Condition Powder is the best treatment which can be resorted to. If worms are the cause of the trouble, give Dr. R. Jennings's Worm Powder.

MANGE.

This is a disease identical with that of itch in man. It is caused by a very minute insect called the *acari equus.* The skin about the neck becomes puckered, the hair comes off in spots, causing scabby patches; there is an intolerable itching, causing the animal to be almost constantly rubbing itself against a post, tree, &c. *Treatment.* —Select a clear, warm day, place the animal in the sun, and, with a scrubbing-brush, wash or scrub him well all over with castile soap and water; when dry, take one quart of sweet-oil and two ounces of kerosene oil, mix them together, wet the brush with the oils, and rub him all over. It does not require to be put on very thick; in fact, it is better not to be so.

SURFEIT.

This is a scurfy eruption of the skin, caused by an unhealthy condition of the blood. *Treatment.*—Give the following :—

R. Socotrine Aloes,   1 oz.
Nitrate Potassa,   1 dr.
Ginger, pulv.,   1 dr.

Mix with molasses, and form a ball; follow this twice a day with Dr. R. Jennings's Condition Powder.

POLL-EVIL.

This disease occurs in horses only when the blood is in a morbid condition: it cannot live in a healthy system. An hereditary predisposition to this disease is frequently transmitted from parent to offspring. Several cases have occurred in my own practice where brood-mares having been affected with this disease, and afterwards having had several colts, and that, too, after the disease had been to all appearances thoroughly healed up, all of which showed the same disease before they arrived at the age of three years. One mare had three colts, another two, and several one, affected in the same way. I do not think better proof of hereditary predisposition can be required. Many mares have this disease, and their colts escape it, simply because they do not have the exciting or immediate cause to develop it. *Treatment.*—The best and quickest means is to cut it out well with the knife, when not too long standing and deeply seated. After such an operation, the wound should be washed with two parts of water to one part of muriatic acid. Open the bowels, and give Dr. R. Jennings's Condition Powder to purify the blood. No corn or cornmeal should be given to the animal. These cases being troublesome, they are best treated by the qualified veterinary surgeon, when he can be obtained.

FISTULA.

This disease is precisely similar to poll-evil, its location only giving it a different name. It occurs more frequently than poll-evil, arises from the same causes, and requires the same treatment. For more full particulars of these diseases, see Dr. R. Jennings's work on "The Horse and his Diseases."

WATER FARCY.

This disease is known by swelling of the legs, sheath, belly, &c. In young horses the parts are hot, and painful to the touch; while in old ones, there appears to be no pain on pressure, but the marks of the fingers will remain behind for some time after. Hand-rubbing and moderate exercise are very necessary, and give in the feed Dr. R. Jenning's Tonic Powder.

LOCKED JAW.

This disease is the result of injuries, such as picking up or running nails in the feet, metallic or other substances taken into and wounding the stomach or intestines; worms are occasionally supposed to give rise to this disease, &c. The first indications of its approach, are a straggling

gait of the hind-legs, which occurs about the
ninth day.   In a few days after, the membrane
nictitans, or haw of the eye, will cover one-third
or more of the eyeball whenever the head is ele-
vated; two or three days -later, the muscles of
the jaw become rigid, the tongue swollen, mouth
full of saliva, nostrils dilated, nose poked out,
and ears erect; the respiration becomes disturbed,
the animal very excitable, bowels constipated; in
turning the horse, he moves without bending his
neck.   The first indication in the treatment is to
remove the patient where he will not be unnecessarily disturbed; open the bowels with the aloes
ball.   This should be done on the first symptoms
being observed, as it is not often successful after
the jaws become set.   Give upon the tongue, in
a little water, ten drops hydrocyanic acid every
two hours; or, the following may be used with
advantage :—

> R. Flemming's Tincture of Aconite, $\frac{1}{2}$ oz.
> Tincture of Belladona, $\frac{1}{2}$ "
> Water,   1 "

Mix; give ten drops every two hours, and apply
Dr. R. Jennings's Sweating Liniment all along
the spine, from the head to the tail.   Keep a pail
of bran-slop before the animal, and put a ball of
aloes in the mouth, as far up as possible; replace
as often as it is dissolved; there is no danger
of giving too much; continue this until the
bowels are opened.   When the foot has been
injured by a nail, open the wound well, and apply

a flaxseed poultice until healthy action takes place.

RHEUMATISM.

This disease is of rare occurrence in this climate; but in Ohio, and some other sections of the United States, it is very common. *Symptoms.*—Stiffness in moving about, the animal is lame first in one leg, then in another, the joints sometimes become swollen, and are painful to the touch, &c. *Treatment.*—The bowels should be opened with the following purge :—

> R. Socotrine Aloes,   1 oz.
> Calomel, $\frac{1}{2}$ dr.
> Pulv. Gentian Root, 2 "

Mix with molasses, and form a ball. Give internally one ounce of pine tar, made into a ball with flour or flaxseed meal, once a day, and bathe the parts with Kerr's East India Liniment, prepared by Jennings & Higgins, Philadelphia, Penna.

CRAMP.

This disease, even when it exists in a severe form, is seldom suspected by the most experienced horsemen, in consequence of the peculiar manner in which the animal is handled. The horse appears perfectly well, eating as usual; but, on attempting to take him out of the stall, he then appears to have lost all power of motion in one of his legs, usually one of the hind ones. On compelling the animal to move, he takes two or three steps naturally enough; when, suddenly, the leg fails to come forward, and is left dragging behind. Hand-rubbing, and bathing the limb with Kerr's East India Liniment, prepared by Jennings & Higgins, will restore the animal in a very short time.

FOUNDER.

The primary cause of this disease is contraction of the hoof, rendering it hard, brittle, and unyielding, in consequence of which, the concussion when the foot is thrown upon the ground when in motion is very much increased. In this condition long drives upon hard roads, bruise the soft and delicate structures within the hoof, in consequence of which the foot becomes sore and fevered. In this condition the animal when warm is often watered, the body is suddenly chilled, causing a determination of blood to the feet, the capillary vessels of the feet become clogged, inflammation is the result, and all the symptoms of founder follow, which are well known to horsemen generally. *Treatment.*—Open the bowels as speedily as possible with the following:

R. Barbadoes Aloes, 1 oz.
Nit. Potassa, 1 dr.
Ginger Pulverized, ½ "

Mix with mucilage gum arabic, and make into a ball. Bleed from the coronet, around the upper part of the foot, at the inside quarter. Foment the feet well with hot water for two or three hours, and then poultice with flaxseed meal, and

in one week's time the animal usually recovers.
After which use Dr. R. Jennings's Hoof Ointment, which will promote healthy action in the
hoof.

PUMICED FEET.

This is a change from the concave sole to a
convex one, in consequence of the absorption of
the lower margin of the os pedis, or bone within
the foot (see Skeleton p. 90), from the inflammation consequent upon neglected founder. Proper
shoeing so as to prevent pressure upon the sole
of the foot, and the use of Dr. R. Jennings's
Hoof Ointment, is all that can be done in these
cases.

NAVICULAR JOINT DISEASE.

This is a disease of frequent occurrence in all
sections of the country. The horse is observed
to point, or advance one foot, sometimes for
months before any lameness is seen. The animal
is at times lame on first going out of the stable,
but recovers from it after travelling a short distance, and may not show it again for days or even
weeks. In some cases it comes on while the
animal is on the road, and disappears in a short
time, in other instances the lameness is continu-
ous. These variations are in consequence of the
difference in the development and intensity of the
disease.

Symptoms.—In its early stages there is no
heat about the foot, no pain upon pressure, no
swelling, the horse picks up the foot naturally

but steps lightly upon it. As the disease increases the animals step becomes short or paddling; particularly is this the case when both feet are involved.

Treatment.—Use Dr. R. Jennings's Sweating Liniment, once a day to the fetlock until the parts are well blistered, then dress with lard; wash the foot every three or four days with castile soap and water, and when dry use the lard. Continue this course until the scurf is all removed, then use the sweating liniment again and dress in like manner. Apply Dr. R. Jennings's Hoof Ointment to the feet every other day. When this treatment fails the frog seton should be resorted to. See Dr. R. Jennings on "The Horse and his Diseases."

OSSIFICATION OF THE LATERAL CARTILAGES.

These are gristly projections from the os pedis, or coffin bone in the foot, arising from contraction of the hoof and other causes. They become inflamed, in consequence of which transformation takes place, converting them into bony masses; in this condition the heels become thickened and in bad cases bulging out considerably; when confirmed the disease is incurable. In its early stage, which is quite difficult to distinguish from navicular joint disease, the use of Dr. R. Jennings's Sweating Liniment, and Hoof Ointment, are indicated.

12

QUITAR.

This disease is often the result of bad corns. Pus or matter is formed within the hoof at the heel, generally upon the inside of the foot, which burrows its way upwards to the top of the hoof where it discharges; in its course upwards it separates the hoof from the soft tissues within. The animal is very lame until the abscess opens at the top of the hoof, when considerable relief is afforded.

Treatment.—Poultice the foot with linseed meal, for several days; cut away all the loosened parts of the hoof, and inject the parts with a solution of sulphate of zinc 2 drachms, to one pint of water, or use nitrate of silver in the same proportions. The foot should be wrapped up to keep dirt from it, and when the parts begin to heal properly, dress once a day with glycerine.

THRUSH.

This is a disease of the frog, caused generally by standing in filthy stables. The almost constant contact of the wet litter causes the frog to become rotten, secreting a very fetid matter in its cleft or division.

Treatment.—Wash the parts clean with soap and water, and while wet sprinkle a small quantity of Dr. R. Jennings's Antiseptic Powder in the cleft, and press it down with a little raw cotton. In a few days repeat if necessary. One application usually is sufficient.

SCRATCHES.

This disease is caused by travelling on muddy roads during a wet season, generally in the spring or fall, or in consequence of an unhealthy condition of the skin causing it to crack in the fetlocks; horsemen understand very well the nature of this disease.

Treatment.—Wash the parts clean with castile soap and water; if the parts are very raw, apply a flaxseed poultice mixed with the following solution. Sulphate of zinc 2 drs. to one pint of water; spread it upon a cloth and place it over the scratches, securing it with a bandage. Continue this for three days; then apply a small quantity of Dr. Rr. Jennings's Antiseptic Powder, or use

> R. Castor Oil,   2 oz.
> Collodion,   1 "

Mix together and apply with a piece of sponge, The parts must be well dried before it is applied. Give internally, Dr. R. Jennings's Condition Powder.

GREASE HEELS.

This is a greasy exudation of a whitish offensive matter from the heels; the skin is hot, tender and swollen; large portions of the skin sometimes slough away, leaving ugly sores to heal.

Treatment.—This must be constitutional as well as local. Give a strong purge, and poultice the parts with linseed meal, in the same manner as recommended in scratches; when the parts assume a healthy action, wash well with castile soap and water, and dress once a day with Dr. R. Jennings's Antiseptic Powder, or use once a week a saturated solution of corrosive sublimate in alcohol; if this latter article is used, do not wash the sores more than once a week with the liquid; it will be necessary, however, to keep the parts clean with castile soap and water.

BONE SPAVIN.

This is a very common disease, located in the hock joint of the horse, (see Skeleton of the Horse, p. 90) arising from strains, sprains, bruises, punctured wounds, in fact anything that will cause inflammation in the hock will produce spavin. See Jennings on "The Horse and his Diseases." Previous to bony deposits being thrown out, bathe the parts when first injured with tincture of arnica; spavin will very frequently be prevented by this simple remedy. When it becomes confirmed spavin, use Dr. R. Jennings's Sweating Liniment.

BLOOD SPAVIN.

This is a puffy swelling upon the inside and front part of the hock, caused by an abundant secretion of synovia or joint oil. It rarely causes lameness or other inconvenience, being nothing more than an eyesore; it may be removed by compresses and cold-water bandages so arranged as to press only upon the swelling. It however requires much care and attention for several months, which few persons are willing to apply.

RING BONE.

This is precisely the same disease as spavin, being seated between the large and small pastern bones, requiring the same treatment as spavin. Both these diseases are slow in their course, requiring generally several months·to overcome the lameness.

SPLINT.

This is an exostosis or bony enlargement, between the cannon and splint bones, showing itself oftener upon the inside of the fore legs than it does upon the outside. A few applications of Dr. R. Jennings's Sweating Liniment will usually drive it away.

CURB.

This is an enlargement of the integument, or in some cases it is caused by bony deposits. In other cases it is the result of breaking down of the hock. This latter is incurable. It is situated at the back part of the hock just below the cap, and often under the most favorable circumstances proves troublesome to manage. Blistering, firing, and setoning are the usual methods of treating this disease. Dr. R. Jennings's Sweating Liniment is the best remedy known to us.

CAPPED HOCK.

This is a puffy swelling of the cap of the hock, containing a serous fluid. It is caused by bruises, in kicking against the side of the stall, and from

12*

other injuries.   Use Dr. R. Jennings's Sweating
Liniment.   Should this fail, resort must be had to
the seton; pass it under the skin the whole length
of the swelling; saturate it with the following:—

R. Cantharides Ointment,   ½ oz.
Spirits of Turpentine,   1 "

Mix together.   Turn the seton once a day, remove
it in two weeks, wash the parts with castile soap
and water, and dress with lard.

SHOULDER STRAIN.

This is one of the most easily detected injuries
to which the horse is liable, as the symptoms are
usually well marked.   If the injury is severe the
shoulder swells.   In consequence of the inflammation, the toe drags upon the ground whenever the
animal moves forwards.   In recent cases foment
the parts well with hot water for half an hour,
then use Kerr's East India Liniment, prepared
by Jennings & Higgins, Veterinary Surgeons.
Tincture of arnica is also a good remedy.

GALLS.

These are generally caused by friction or unequal pressure from the saddle, collar, &c.   Bathe
the parts with the following: it is the best preparation known to us.

R. Tincture of Aloes,   1 oz.
Tincture of Myrrh,   2 "

Mix, and use two or three times a day.

WARTS.

| These are fibrous or seedy fungoid growths, occurring in various parts of the body. In colts they frequently present themselves in great numbers about the nose. Treatment : Let them alone when about the nose of colts; in horses, they should be removed with the knife, or by a string tied tightly round them, and kept there until they slough away. Permanganate of potash, as a caustic, is an excellent remedy.

CASTRATING COLTS.

This operation, to say the least, is a barbarous one, necessity only justifying its performance. This fact admitted, it becomes us, as rational beings, to perform the operation in such a manner as involves the least risk, the least pain, and the least inconvenience to the animal operated upon. Castration is one of the most ancient operations known to man. The different methods which have from time to time been practised, we will not consider in this little work, but will be content with mentioning the operation introduced into the United States, by the author, several years ago. This consists in removing the testicles by means of the *acraseur*, an instrument invented for the removal of hemorrhoides (piles) in man. The advantages of this operation over all others are, First : it is safer, better, less painful, more scientific, and less barbarous than any other at present known. Second : the wounds heal quickly, seldom requiring more than two weeks, and usually not more than one. Third : the operation is less troublesome to the skilful operator, as well as to the owner of the animal, as the colt is done with as soon as it is let up, no after treatment as a general thing being required, as in other methods, such as keeping the scrotum open, &c. Fourth : usually little or no swelling takes place, the animal being scarcely affected in any preceptible way by the operation. Fifth : there is no more hemorrhage than by any other operation. An experience of twenty years' active practice justifies me in making the above assertions, averaging over one hundred operations a year. Where a sufficient number of colts are obtained in any section of the country, to justify an excursion, the services of Dr. R. Jennings may be obtained to perform the operations by addressing him at Philadelphia, Pa.

GLANDERS.

This subject being one of great interest at the present time to horsemen and the public generally, and having in connection with the Philadelphia Society for promoting Agriculture, distributed 2500 copies of my pamphlet on Glanders gratuitously, and the applications being several thousands more than could be supplied, induces the author to republish it in connection with this work.

GLANDERS.

———◆———

The sales of condemned government horses in New Jersey and adjacent states, having introduced into our county and immediate vicinity the terrible scourge known as "glanders," I conceive it my imperative duty to warn you in time of the danger which is threatening our community.

If the experience of a veterinary surgeon, who has devoted twenty years of his life to the relief of the noblest animal in the gift of Providence, is not sufficient to excite your sympathy and even your fears, I am convinced that the following reports, based upon evidential facts and undoubted authority, will attain that object.

You will see the proofs that "glanders" is a disease without remedy, positively incurable, *extremely contagious*, easily *communicated to man*, and that every day human life is sacrificed to incredulity and ignorance !

GLANDERS.

DEFINITION.—Glanders consists in a discharge, from one or both nostrils, of matter which by transfer or inoculation will produce the disease

(141)

in another animal (of the equine or human species), and which discharge is sooner or later
accompanied by vascular injection and chancrous
ulceration of the schneiderian membrane, by
tumefaction of the submaxillary lymphatic glands,
and by farcy.—*Percival.*

SYMPTOMS.—A discharge of matter from one
or both nostrils, enlargement of one or both sub-
maxillary glands. When one nostril only is
affected, the corresponding gland is almost invariably found enlarged. The schneiderian membrane (lining of the nose) is generally of a pale
or leaden hue, and sometimes ulcerations are
visible on its surface. The discharge usually
sticks to the nostrils, and is sometimes white and
thick, but oftener of a grayish aspect. A discharge from the nostrils, and the appearance
of ulceration, is not alone sufficient to establish
the presence of the disease; for these ulcerations
are sometimes produced by the acrid nature
of the discharge from catarrh. In the first stage
of the disease, there is a discharge from one
nostril only of a whitish humor, which is incon-
siderable, except when the horse has been exercised
for some time. There is an increased redness
of the membrane within the nostrils. The swelling of the glands under the jaw is on the same
side as the affected nostril. The horse's coat
appears healthy, and the animal in good condition.

The symptoms of glanders, arising from communication with a glandered horse, are different
from those of glanders produced by bad proven-

der, excessive exertion, &c. In the former, the discharge is from one nostril only, or much more from one than from the other; and there is no cough or other symptom of catarrh or cold, or any other disorder. In the latter, on the contrary, there is cough, either dry or moist; and it is preceded by loss of appetite, or falling off in appetite, and depression of spirits.

The symptoms of the second stage are, the altered appearance of the nasal discharge, which has become more glutinous, and adheres to the edges of the nostril, with a contraction and partial closing of the nostril, with increased tenderness of the swelling under the jaw, which adheres more closely to the jaw-bone; the discharge is somewhat streaked with blood, and of an offensive smell. The discharge is now from both nostrils. There is a slight tumefaction of the under eyelid, a swelling or elevation of the bones of the nose or forehead. Loss of appetite, debility, cough, and swelling of the legs and sheath, and sometimes lameness without any apparent cause, chancres or ulcerations within the nostrils, great tenderness of the glands under the jaw, which now adhere close to the jaw-bone, a small discharge of matter from the inner corner of the eye. When these symptoms appear, the disease soon proceeds to a fatal termination. The above symptoms are not all peculiar to glanders, but may occur in strangles, peripneumony, and pleurisy. The glutinous discharge, the swelling of the glands under the jaw, and the ulceration within the nostrils, are symptoms which occur in the above diseases, as well as in glanders.

Although the disease is here divided into the first and second stages, it is not essential that in each case the former should precede the latter, for sometimes the acute only is present, and the horse speedily dies, if not destroyed. In other instances, the acute stage may be succeeded by the sub-acute. It may, however, be observed, that the first stage never ends in death, but it is always in the second stage that the disease proves fatal. Besides these stages, glanders sometimes assumes a still more insidious appearance, in which the discharge is so slight, and the enlarged gland so trivial, as not only to deceive the ignorant, but often to mislead the well-instructed practitioner. The discharge is thin, and appears no more than a slight increase of the natural discharge, and the sub-maxillary swelling is no larger than a bean, though hard and indurated. Such cases as these have proved of irreparable injury to many horse proprietors, from the symptoms not being sufficiently urgent to excite alarm ; and when a veterinary surgeon has given his opinion that such case was one of glanders, there have not been wanting plenty of farriers and others who have altogether contemned such an opinion, and, for a time at least, have exulted over their own superior sagacity. Mr. James Turner relates a striking instance of this, in which his advice was disregarded, and a horse, with these insidious appearances, was allowed to mix with other horses, to several of which he communicated the disease in the course of a few months.— *White's Veterinary Art.*

The most common cause of this disease is the impure air of close, ill-ventilated, damp, and filthy stables, acting injuriously upon the organs of respiration, destroying the constitution, debilitating the system, rendering it susceptible to the attack of disease. Neglected catarrh, strangles, &c., sometimes terminate in glanders; hard work and bad provender, together with sudden changes from exposure to cold and wet weather, to hot stables, &c., are likewise regarded as among the causes; contagion is the most common of all causes, the disease being readily communicated from one animal to another by it.

" The city of Lyons, France, must always contain a great number of glandered horses, on account of the dampness of the situation and climate, and it being a public market for horses. The garrison at Lyons generally has its share of this disease. During this year the mildness of the winter, and the heat of the spring and summer, have prevented circumstances less favorable than usual, to the development of this malady; therefore, with the exception of horses from the garrison, and which had been long kept in the infirmary at the barracks before they were sent to us, we have had very few cases of glanders, compared with several preceding years; yet notwithstanding these favorable circumstances, we are compelled to acknowledge that it has been

13

as rebellious to treatment as ever. Our means of cure have always possessed too little power, seeing that when ulceration of the pituitary (of the nose) membrane begins to appear, the lungs and constitution of the animal have undergone a modification which it is difficult to remove.

"The greater part of the animals that have gone from us, apparently cured of glanders, have speedily relapsed when they have been subjected to hard work, or have been exposed to neglect or privation." — *Extract from the Report of the Veterinary College of Lyons,* 1834 *and* 1835.

Mr. W. Percival, in his "Hippopathology," gives us the following facts as the result of his own experience :—

1. "That farcy and glanders, which constitute the same disease, are propagated through the medium of stabling, and this we believe to be the more usual way in which diseases are communicated from horse to horse.

2. "That infected stabling may harbor and retain the infection for months, or even years; and although by thoroughly cleansing and making use of disinfecting means, the contagion may be destroyed, yet it would not be wise to occupy such stables *immediately* after such supposed or alleged disinfection.

3. "That the virus, or poison of glanders, may lie for months in a state of incubation in the horse's constitution before the disease breaks out. Of this we have had most positive evidence.

4. "That when a stable of horses becomes

contaminated, the disease often makes fearful ravages among them before it quits; and it is only after a period of several months exemption from all disease of the kind, that a clean bill of health can be rendered."

FARCY.

This I regard as an incipient stage of glanders, or as a type of the same fatal malady, and is to a certain extent curable. Experiments prove that the virus from a farcied horse will produce glanders by inoculation in a sound one, and that the glandered matter will in like manner produce farcy. There are two distinct varieties or stages of farcy; one, which is called button farcy, is altogether superficial, being confined to the lymphatic vessels of the skin, and readily yields to medical treatment; the other variety makes its appearance in the extremities, generally upon the inside of the hind-legs, which become completely engorged; but the swelling is very different from the ligamentary thickening, or from œdema, being very uneven or lumpy, excessively tender, and painful to the touch. Small abscesses are formed, which at first discharge a healthy pus, but soon ulcerate, and discharge a thin sanious matter. These abscesses first make their appearance on the inside of the hind-legs, and then on the fore ones in like manner; the neck and lips come next in turn, and they may appear in all parts of the body, when glanders will begin to manifest itself.

Stonehenge says: " Farcy appears to depend upon the development of the same poison as in glanders; but the attempt at elimination is made in the skin, instead of the mucous membrane lining the nose. A horse inoculated with glanders may exhibit farcy, and *vice versa.*"

" Farcy usually shows itself first by one or two small hard knots in the skin called ' farcy buds;' these soon soften and contain a small quantity of pus; but, as this is rapidly absorbed, the lymphatics which convey it into the circulation inflame; and at a short distance another bud is formed, &c. In process of time the general system suffers, as in glanders, and the horse dies, a miserable, worn-out object. No treatment can be relied on to cure the disease; and, as it is equally contagious with glanders, every farcied horse ought at once to be destroyed. The hard nature of the buds, and the thickened lymphatics extending like cords between, clearly make known the nature of the disease."

Glanders Contagious.—This brings us to the more important part of our subject, and places us upon our guard, so as to prevent us as far as possible exposing ourselves to such a calamity. The time which glanders appears after inoculation is very uncertain; it may be a few days, or it may be several months, varying according to circumstances and the condition of the animal. Glanders has been known to remain dormant in the system for a period of two or three years previous to its being developed.

"*The main cause is contagion.*—I now approach, gentlemen, not without hesitation, but without fear, the grand cause of Glanders—Contagion. I advisedly call it 'the grand cause,' for I believe that I shall be able to render it probable that glanders arises oftener from contagion than from any other source. I know that our continental neighbors deny the contagiousness of glanders altogether; but they do not, and cannot deny that the disease does follow contact, and often mere proximity of situation. When they tell me that it is not the disease that is communicated, but a mere predisposition, a greater aptitude in the frame generally, or some part of it, to be affected by the usual causes of glanders, I cannot but regard this as the merest quibbling. I take the broad fact, that a glandered horse being inadvertently admitted into a stable, some of his companions, after awhile, become glandered too. The stable had previously, and for many years—nay, from the very time of its erection—been free from the disease, and no alteration, whatever, has taken place in the system of management: a glandered horse finds his way thither, in a few months the whole team is glandered. When in the face of this, a person tells me that it was not the disease which was communicated, but a facility of being acted upon by certain agents, I regard it as a species of quibbling, unworthy of a scientific pathologist; and I deprecate the injury which may be done to the agricultural community by the broad assertion,

13 *

thus ridiculously and falsely explained, that
glanders is not contagious.   One point, however,
is established, I think,—that glanders is far more
contagious than many have supposed; Mr.
Turner's mare destroyed four of her companions.
The poor Widow at Paddington had her stable
perfectly emptied by the disease; and I will venture to say, that there is not a district throughout
the kingdom, in which some farmer, by the loss
of a considerable proportion, or the greater part
of his team, has not had sufficient proof of the
contagiousness of glanders.   The cause of this
doubt with regard to the frequent communication
of the disease by inoculation, seems to have arisen
from ignorance of its insidious nature.   When
glanders appears, and the horse has, for several
weeks or months, scarcely been exposed to the
possibility of contagion, it has at once been con-
cluded that the disease was generated in him by
some assigned or unknown recent cause.   It has
now, however, been proved to us that the disease
may exist and may be communicated to others,
when, for many months, there has been nothing
to excite suspicion in the mind of the groom or
the owner; and when the candid veterinary surgeon acknowledges, that, had not the circumstances been pointed out to him, it would probably
have escaped his observation.   The truth of the
matter is then, that every horse that passes
through a fair, or is baited at an inn, or even
travels the common public road, may be infected
without the rider's or owner's knowledge or

slightest suspicion. A glandered stallion neighed at a mare that was separated from him by a double hedge and a deep lane; the virus was wafted across by the wind, and she became diseased, and died. It is impossible for any one to say, except there be some plain and manifest cause for the generation of the disease, that any horse did not receive it by infection. There would be a degree of presumption in the assertion which the calm inquirer after truth should not display. The opinion of our ancestors, from time out of date, had taught us to beware of glanders as a contagious as well as a fatal disease. Let us not, without incontestable proof, abandon that which for ages was never doubted. There is not a circumstance that has been productive of half so much loss to the agriculturist, and the proprietor of horses, as this too frequently and too positively repeated assertion of the non-contagiousness of glanders. Many thousands of pounds would not cover the *annual* loss. A case occurred about two years ago, and not a very great way from this metropolis. A gentleman had a team of farm-horses, almost unrivalled for activity and strength. One of them exhibited symptoms of incipient glanders. A newly arrived young veterinarian was consulted as to the propriety of preventing all further mischief, and cutting short the affair, by destroying the diseased animal. 'Oh! by no means,' said he; 'there is not the danger about glanders which some foolish people imagine; you well ventilate

your stables, and let there be no animal poison
lurking there from air that has been breathed
over and over again, and I will answer for it,
your other horses are safe enough; there is not
one horse in a thousand that *catches* glanders.'
The gentleman was somewhat surprised, and ex-
pressed a little doubt about the matter; but, the
young theorist producing chapter and verse in
elucidation of his point, he suffered himself to be
over-persuaded; and in less than a twelvemonth
he had not a sound horse upon his farm."—
Youatt's Lectures at the University of London,
1832.

The glanders is a disease of the horse tribe, com-
municable to man and other animals. It is chiefly
manifested by unhealthy suppuration of the mucous membrane of the nasal cavities, and pustular
eruptions on the skin, and unhealthy abscesses
in the lymphatic system.—*Druitt's Surgery.*

The instant that there is any appearance of it,
the horse should be immediately removed to a
place by itself, as this malady is exceedingly
infectious; and from want of due caution, when
even a suspicion is entertained, the most dis-
astrous consequences have been the result.—
Brown's Farriery.

GLANDERS.—A disease in horses, attended
with a copious discharge of mucus from the nose.
It is needless to endeavor to describe the various
attempts which have been made to cure this
almost invariably fatal disorder. But the farmer
must avoid a common error of confounding ulcer-

ation of the membrane of the nose with glanders, for the symptoms are very similar. The farmer will do well, as soon as he finds a horse attacked with this disease, to place him by himself, give him green food, and thoroughly whitewash the stable from which he is taken, for it is a most contagious disease.—*American Farmer's Encyclopedia.*

· Two thorough-bred colts, yearlings, that had never been broke or put into a stable, were affected with the glanders to a violent degree. It was considered by the proprietor as a very extraordinary circumstance that having never been kept with any other horse, these colts should have been attacked with the disease. On inquiry, however, the author found that a canal ran on the side of the field in which these colts were kept, and that upon one occasion, some boatmen had been detected in turning their horses to graze in the same field; and hence a very fair presumption arose that the contagion was communicated in that way.—*Lawrence.*

That the glanders is contagious, has been clearly and indisputably proved by numerous experiments, and the manner in which it is propagated has likewise been satisfactorily demonstrated. The great number of horses that have been destroyed by glanders, especially in the army, and in the establishments where great numbers of horses are kept, has excited particular attention to the subject, especially in France and Italy, where many attempts were made in the beginning of the last century to discover a remedy for it.—*Skeavington.*

"It is a remarkable circumstance," says Mr. White, "that glanders cannot be communicated by applying the matter which is discharged from the nose of a glandered horse to the nostrils of a sound one, unless there be an open wound or sore, even though a piece of lint, soaked in the matter, be put up the nostrils, and kept in contact with the pituitary membrane for a short time; or even if the matter be thrown up the nostrils with a syringe. But, if the smallest quantity of matter be applied in the way of inoculation, either to the membrane of the nostrils, or to any part of the body, a glanderous ulcer will be produced, from which farcy buds and corded lymphatics will proceed. After a few weeks the poison will get into the circulation, and the horse will be completely glandered. The circumstance of glanders not being communicated by applying matter to the nostril, enables us to account for a horse escaping the disorder, as he sometimes does, after being put into a glandered stable, or standing by the side of a glandered horse. I am inclined to believe that the disorder is more readily caught by eating the glanderous matter mixed with oats or hay, than by drinking it with water, as in the former case it is so intimately mixed with the food in mastication. M. St. Bell placed two sound horses by a glandered horse, drinking out of the same pail, and eating out of the same manger. One of the sound horses was six years old, and just taken from grass; the other nine years old, and taken from regular work. The first showed evident signs of glanders at the expiration of thirty-four days; it fully declared itself in the second at the end of six weeks."

John Gamgee, Professor in the Edinburgh Veterinary College, says : " Horses undoubtedly affected with this dreadful malady should be destroyed as soon as the disease is satisfactorily diagnosed. Various mineral tonics have been vaunted as specifics, but we cannot conceive on what principle animals should be allowed to live, endangering the life of those around them, with no benefit to themselves.

"A glandered horse may contaminate the air of a stable to such a degree, that horses breathing the same air may become infected with the disease, although the infected may never come in contact with the infecting horse. Fortunately glanders is not so infectious as some other diseases to which horses are liable, otherwise the breed would soon become extinct."—*Veterinarian*, 1833.

" GLANDERS.—We have had about the same number of glandered horses as in the last year; and we must repeat, that in spite of all the care that has been bestowed upon them, and the strict attention which has been paid to the administration of medicines the most likely to have a good effect, and the power of which has been vaunted by others, we are not able to relate a single case of the complete cure of glanders. Seven horses were returned to their owners apparently cured—all the recognisable symptoms of the disease had disappeared; six of them were, after some months, returned to us more decidedly glandered than they were before; they were destroyed. The seventh has now been away three months; but we reckon upon seeing him again about the same time as the others, and in the same state as that in which they returned."— *From the proceedings of the Veterinary College, Alfort, France,* 1833-4.

"ACUTE GLANDERS.—MM. Renault and Bowley have continued their researches on this disease. An inquiry into the nature of this malady, its symptoms, and, more especially, its contagious property, has acquired increasing interest since its transmissibility from the horse to the human being has been lately proved in so many instances. MM. Renault and Bowley have arrived at the following results: Acute glanders is contagious by inoculation from horse to horse. Every experiment of the last and the present year has given this positive constant result. Without a single exception, the symptoms of the infection of glanders have appeared in the inoculated animals from the third to the fifth day, and death has ensued between the tenth and fifteenth days."—*Veterinarian.*

In the year 1861, my attention was called to seventeen horses, the property of Mr. E. K. B., of Felton, Delaware, who, some six months previous, had purchased a horse at the horse-auction in Philadelphia. This animal was supposed to have a slight attack of what is commonly called "distemper." In a short time some of Mr. B.'s other horses showed symptoms of the same disease, several of which died. Mr. B., becoming alarmed at his repeated losses, called in my assistance. I found (if my memory serves me right) five of the seventeen horses glandered, three of which I ordered killed. The others which had not shown symptoms of disease, I ordered to be at once removed from the stable, so as to prevent all possible communication between them and those in which the disease was not fully developed. Mr. B. loaned Mr. H., a neighbor, one of his horses to work in a lumber team; soon after which the disease made its appearance in Mr. H.'s stock of ten horses. My attention was called to these animals, also, several of which I found laboring from the same fatal malady. Two of these animals in which the disease was fully developed I ordered killed. Removing my residence from Philadelphia to Bordentown, N. J., about this time, I lost sight of these cases, and have not since heard from them.

Soon after the present rebellion broke out, one of my old customers, Mr. H., who kept a livery-stable in Cherry street, Philadelphia, was doing a thriving business, and having a number of the finest horses in the city kept there. Two army horses were put up for the night at that stable. No appearance of disease was observed about them

14

One of these horses occupied a stall near to that occupied by Dr. L.'s horse, which was valued at $300. Soon after this visit, Dr. L.'s horse showed evidence of ozena, which rapidly degenerated into glanders; the animal was killed. Case No. 2, valued at $500, the property of Mr. D., fell a victim to this fatal disease, and was also killed. Case 3, valued at $300, belonging to Mr. B., also became glandered and was destroyed; together with six other animals, all valuable and highly prized by their owners. This calamity fell heavily on Mr. H., who in consequence was compelled to relinquish the business for some other occupation. This stable has since been torn out, the walls picked, remodelled, and it is once more in successful operation, with new stock and a new proprietor, who it is to be hoped will meet with better fortune.

In 1854, when inspector of the Philadelphia Mutual Live-Stock Insurance Co., I was called to examine a fine gray horse belonging to Mr. W., of the Western Exchange Hotel, recently insured for $300, which policy had just expired. Mr. W. asserted that the animal had only a slight cold, but was getting better: on examining the animal, however, I pronounced him glandered, which the owner was loth to believe: in order to satisfy him of the correctness of my diagnosis, I called in T. J. Corbyn and the late W. W. Fraley, veterinary surgeons, both of whom confirmed my opinion. Mr. W., not wishing to destroy the horse, desired me to experiment with him in

order, if possible, to save his life. Some two
weeks subsequently, a farmer stopping at the
hotel, supposing himself well acquainted with
such diseases, offered Mr. W. $75 for the horse,
asserting at the same time that it was only the
distemper that ailed him, and he could cure any
horse of that disease. Mr. W. immediately consulted me in regard to the propriety of selling
the horse: my advice was, under the circumstances, to clear himself of all responsibility.
The result was the horse was sold. Some six
months later, I learned that the horse was dead,
together with two other animals belonging to the
same unfortunate purchaser.

Sometime last spring, Mr. P., residing near
Pemberton, New Jersey, purchased a horse which
showed, as he thought, symptoms of "distemper;"
for some reason or other, Mr. P. did not keep
this animal long, but sold him to a Mr. J., residing some two miles distant. Soon after Mr.
P. parted with this animal, he sent another horse
belonging to him to me for examination which
had been previously treated for nasal gleet.
This animal I unhesitatingly pronounced glandered, and recommended his destruction; the
animal, however, died in a few days, since which
time another of Mr. P.'s horses has shown symptoms of the same disease. Subsequently I was
called to see the horses belonging to Mr. J., who
had lost three animals since the purchase of Mr.
P.'s horse, and had two more sick with the same
fatal disease, all of which had been treated in

the same manner as were those of Mr. P. I found these animals also glandered, and ordered one of them to be killed; the other died, making seven animals thus far inoculated by one glandered horse. These cases show the necessity existing for competent veterinary surgeons who have been regularly educated in the same manner as are human medical practitioners.

In my private correspondence with veterinary surgeons, I learn that glanders is rapidly spreading all over the country. Dr. Isaiah Michener, of Bucks county, Pa., writes to me as follows: "I have just returned from a trip to see two cases of laryngitis, accompanied with enlargement of the sub-maxillary gland, and adhesiveness of the matter discharged from the nose, that led me to suspect that glanders might have been lying dormant in the system, until provoked to a development by the above disease; but more anon. One other case seen to-day was bought at a sale of condemned government horses; he is discharging freely from both nostrils; no enlargement of the glands or evidence of the schneiderian membrane being affected; still I consider that glanders is lurking in his system, in the form of tubercles in the lungs. I was called last spring to see a case of glanders that a Mr. —— had been treating for several weeks, telling the owner at every visit that there was no glanders about the horse, and he would cure him. The case was well defined, and no man who knows anything about the symptoms of glanders could for a moment be in doubt. This week I was called to see another case, also an army horse, treated by the same party for three months, assuring the owner that there was no danger; as he did not have the glanders, because the dis-. charge was from the right nostril, together with other *say saes* equally absurd. The owner, strangely impressed with the idea of glanders, removed the animal from his other stock, notwithstanding his professional adviser assured him there was no danger, and that he was unnecessarily cautious.

"I was called last week to see a horse which the owner said had the distemper, but on examination I found it was glanders, which the owner was very unwilling to believe, and insisted that I should give him medicine. This horse was also from the army."

G. W. Bowler, veterinary surgeon, Cincinnati, informs me that glanders is spreading at a fearful rate since the sale of government horses in that vicinity.

T. B. Rayner, veterinary surgeon, of Chestnut Hill, Philadelphia, informs me that many cases have recently come under his notice.

On passing up Filbert street, Philadelphia, the other day, in company with R. McClure, V. S., and several of the students of the Veterinary College, my attention was attracted to an army horse belonging to the 20th cavalry regiment: this animal had tetanus (locked jaw) in its worst form; tied to the same post was another animal

14*

badly affected with farcy glanders—that is, the two stages of glanders combined. These horses were waiting their turn to be shod at a shoeing shop in the neighborhood. In close proximity to these animals were some ten or a dozen other horses, the owners of which were perfectly innocent of the danger in which their animals were placed. Qualified veterinary surgeons in the army would prevent all such occurrences. The horse with locked jaw cannot be used for any purpose, and it would not be a matter of surprise if he did not reach his camp.

I have condemned several horses as glandered during the last few months, some of which were afterwards sold, with, of course, a guilty knowledge, to other parties innocent of the nature of the disease. Such men should be held responsible by law for all damage resulting from such a sale. Did these parties know the weight of the responsibility which rests upon them, they would not for a few paltry dollars sacrifice the property and often the lives of their fellow-men.

R. McClure, V. S., says : " The symptoms of glanders are to be studied, not with a view to its cure, which is at all times dangerous to attempt, as there is the risk of contagion to him who attempts it; but with a view of ascertaining and diagnosing truly that it is glanders, that being all that can repay for the trouble, in order that the animal be destroyed at once, as it is not fit to live upon the face of the earth, with contamination following in its wake.

BEWARE OF GLANDERED HORSES.

There is one point upon which we desire to caution our readers—a point which we deem all-important, and which, we trust, will challenge their earnest and prompt consideration. As rapidly as army horses, whether from disease or accident, become unfit for service, they are put up at auction and sold to the highest bidder. As the prices obtained for them are not large, many farmers are induced to make purchases. It is now a well-established fact, that that most loathsome, contagious, and fatal disease, the glanders, prevails to a large extent among the army horses, and that, of those already sold, a great many have been afflicted with it. These glandered animals have been distributed through every section of the country, and it is a notorious fact that there are now ten cases of this dangerous disease among our farm-horses, where there was a single one two years since. What is to be done in such a case? Shall this introduction of a most pestilent disease be permitted to go on? If it be, we may confidently look forward to the almost complete extermination of our horses; for the facility with which the disease communicates itself from one animal to another, and the speedy and fatal termination of the disease, where it is the result of contagion, point to no other result. The government should at once take this matter in hand, and remedy the crying evil, by ordering the immediate killing of every glandered horse in the army.—*Culturist.*

GLANDERED HORSES.

Written for the "National Union," by G. W. Bowler, Veterinary Surgeon, Cincinnati.

In consequence of the many reports received of the increased number of glandered horses in various parts of the United States, it becomes our duty to make some inquiries as to the cause of such a malignant and fatal disease, as well as to use such measures as will mitigate it. I have no doubt but that it can be accounted for in the following manner: We are well aware of the bad treatment which the horses belonging to the army receive, not only in the manner in which they are stabled, but in the feeding of the animal; and where a large number of horses are crowded together, without any regard to cleanliness or protection from the cold and wet, disease in some form must necessarily ensue. Thousands of valuable animals are annually being sacrificed in the United States army, through ignorance, which might otherwise have been saved, was there but some little system adopted to prevent it; but, where hundreds of animals are crowded together, regardless of proper shelter from the weather, and under the control of persons who know little, if anything, about the proper care of horses, why, nothing short of disease of a malignant character can be expected. The very plan to propagate such diseases as glanders and farcy is daily practised among horses of the United States Army; for it is well known by all medical men, that undue exposure to the weather, transition from heat to cold, improper feeding, uncleanliness, and bad ventilation, are the very means to bring about such diseases as glanders, farcy, and other diseases of a debilitating character.

One day the animals, as I have been informed by persons in the Government service, will have more food placed before them than they can possibly consume, and probably for several days previous they have been on the verge of starvation, eager to devour almost anything within their reach, not excepting the fences they were tied to. How then can anything else be expected, but a great many of them will die from disease of the bowels or stomach?

Catarrhal affections are very naturally to be expected amongst a large number of horses exposed to the various changes of the weather; but do not a great many of these affections, for want of proper treatment, run into glanders? That they do, I have not the shadow of a doubt; but as the government does not employ competent persons to examine the horses regularly, why the disease runs on; the glandered horse coming in contact with his associates transfers it to them, and thus the disease is spread throughout the camp. Furthermore than this, not only are the horses in danger of communicating the disease to their own species, but are in danger of transferring the disease to the persons who have charge of them, and who little know the fearful risk they are incurring, of becoming inoculated by the poisonous matter. A simple scratch on the hand, should a portion of the glanded matter come in contact with it, would be sufficient to inoculate a person, the result of which would be, a most terrible death.

For the special benefit of such persons as may be employed about the Government horses, I will give a brief account of the nature, cause, and diagnosis of glanders, in order to put the inexperienced on their guard. Glanders is a disease of a most loathsome and malignant character, occurring far more frequently in the horse than any other animal; still I am inclined to believe that it rages with far more violence when communicated to the ass or mule, than it does even in the horse. Another important fact in regard to the loathsome disease, and which ought always to be borne in mind by those employed about stables, where the disease is likely to exist, is that it is not confined to the equine species, but is readily communicated to the human being. The only domestic animals which appear to be free from contamination are the ox and the sheep, which do not appear to take the disease even by inoculation.

GLANDERS IN THE HUMAN BEING.

The path of propriety and of duty evidently is to put the farmer and horse-proprietor on their guard. The experience of every age, and I would say of every man who has seen country practice, teaches him that a glandered horse can rarely remain long among sound ones without serious mischief ensuing. It is affirmed that glanders is communicated to the human being. That a loathsome and fatal disease results from inoculation with the matter of glanders is undoubted : I am aware, indeed, of one case which goes a great way towards establishing the identity of the disease. One of the feeders in the Badsworth hunt cut himself while preparing a farcied leg for the hounds; he died within a week. A day or two before his death an ass was inoculated with the matter from some of the sores that broke out about him, and died, evidently glandered.— *Youatt's Lectures.*

A man aged twenty-three was admitted into St. Thomas's Hospital; he complained of much pain in the head and became delirious, to mitigate which, leeches were applied to the forehead; he then spoke of wandering and acute pains everywhere, indicating some rheumatic affection; a tumor appeared upon the hand and another on the foot, seemingly of a gangrenous nature; the pain in the head would again return attended by delirium, so that he was compelled to be strapped on his bed; and all the while his flesh was wasting and his strength diminishing. On questioning the poor fellow, it was ascertained that he had had a glandered horse under his care a month before, and that the discharge from the nose had come upon his hands. The case was now sufficiently plain; but the patient was too far gone to admit of the slightest hope. Previous to his death he said, "I am dying, I shall die soon, but I shall die happy;—I know now I am glandered—I shall die as my horses do—I shall die happy."—*Veterinarian*, 1833.

A case is mentioned in the "*Lancet*" of 1834, of a Mr. Norbrook, who punctured a blister on his knee with a lance with which he had previously been bleeding a horse; some of the blood remained on the blade, from this he was inoculated, and died a horrid death.

"This school has, in the year just expiring, added another mournful case to those previously recorded in the hospitals of the biped, of the communication of glanders to the human being." —*Alfort College Record*, 1838.

Dr. Barham, of Truro, reports a case of glanders in the "*Veterinarian*" of 1840, in the person of Joseph Pascoe, aged 22, resulting in death.

A young man named P. Kelley, aged twenty, was admitted into Richmond hospital on the 26th August 1838. On admission his face presented that peculiar aspect which is so characteristic of glanders; the left half was very much swollen, tense, and shining, the redness fading away gradually and becoming lost in the surrounding integuments. He stated that he had always been healthy, and when questioned as to the nature of his occupation, said that he had been employed for the last four months in attending horses that were glandered; he did not recollect that he had a wound or sore on either hand; he had not drank out of any vessel used by the horses, nor had he slept in the stable. He died on the 29th. — *Dublin Journal of Medical Science*, 1841.

Mr. Rocher, medical student at the hospital of Necker, was charged with the dressing of a patient affected, first, with chronic farcy, and subsequently with acute glanders, under which he died. In a few days Mr. Rocher showed evidences of the disease, and died glandered, six-teen days from the commencement of the disease. —*Lancet*, 1841.

In the latter part of May I was requested to see Andrew Foot, aged thirty-six, who presented all the symptoms of glanders. I could not dis-cover any appearances of his having been inocu-lated, but having seen a glandered horse some time since, and thinking the above unfortunate case so much resembled that of this horse, I was induced to inquire of the owner whether there was anything the matter with either of his horses, when he told me that one of them was laid up with a bad cold. On examining the ani-mal it proved to be a decided case of glanders. The horse died in ten days afterwards; Mr. Foot died also.—*Provincial Medical Journal.*

In the hospitals at Paris, according to the ac-counts of the medical journals, the cases of glan-ders among men have been less frequent than in any preceding years. Sidon, a veterinary sur-geon, published a paper in France, in which he stated that glanders was transmissible from the horse to man, causing the worst kinds of ulcers.

15

He mentions an instance in which a horse was affected by the disease from a farrier who had a glandered sore on his hand, which came in contact with the animal while he was giving it a ball. The man and the horse both died with the disease.

A groom, named Provost, slept in a stable at Paris, occupied by a glandered horse. Some days after the death of the animal Provost was attacked with the same disease and died.

Mr. Hamerton, surgeon to the Castle-town Dispensary, has placed upon record three cases of acute glanders in the human subject, all running the same course, and terminating fatally, and all traceable to the same cause, *i. e.*, contagion from a diseased horse.— *Veterinarian*, 1843.

A vine-grower, in drenching a glandered horse, was bitten on the cheek; fifteen days after he died glandered.— *Vet.* 1844.

The patient, whom I saw several times during the progress of the malady, was Thomas Whittaker, whose case was clearly one of inoculation. The poor fellow was bald-headed, and received a slight scratch on his scalp which cost him his life. He recollected wiping the perspiration off his head with his dirty hands; and as the scratch in his scalp first showed the true character of a farcy ulcer, there can be little doubt as to the inoculation having taken place at the time of skinning the farcied horse. He survived the inoculation twenty-one days. Robert Pick, an old, faithful, and I believe, valued, servant to the gentleman

who owned the farcied pony, was the subject of
the second lamentable case, which is considered
one of infection; and the infection is supposed
to have been conveyed by the fetid breath of the
animal, while the poor man was in the act of
giving some mucilage of linseed to the pony a
few hours before his death. A few hours after
the death of the pony, Dick complained of being
unwell, and of having pain in his knee. At first
the pain was regarded as rheumatism, but ulti-
mately proved to be that of farcy, as that disease
showed itself in its true character and virulence,
which ended the suffering patient's life on the
twenty-second day after he had inhaled the fetid
breath of the animal.— *Vet.* 1846.

"Within the last quarter two veterinary surgeons—one residing in Walworth, and the other
in Wolverhampton—are reported as having died
from inoculation of glanders. This terrible disease is not often seen in Scotland, but very frequently in England, and still more so in Ireland.
From the latter circumstance, the malady is often
found to be imported about the west coast of
Scotland. London has always been renowned
for the prevalence of glanders among omnibus,
cab, and other horses. A very strict supervision
is maintained, and all glandered horses are destroyed when discovered; but nevertheless, we
can state on good authority that the omnibus
horses of London have suffered very severely
from this disease, and do so still. The partial
measures adopted by companies are not sufficient

to eradicate it, and the "glandered night team" is not altogether a thing of the past. The danger to human life is so great that we feel happy to seize an opportunity to urge the adoption of the most effectual measures for the suppression of any practice which tends to prolong the life of the glandered horse."

Another case, as published in the *Herald of Reform*," is as follows:—

"Mr. J. Burns, a grocer, in Baltimore, died a horrid death in that city, a few days ago, in consequence of poison communicated to his system from a horse afflicted with glanders. During the administration of medicine Mr. B. thrust into the animal's mouth his hand, a finger of which had been previously cut, and the flesh laid open. Through this wound the virus was absorbed, and mortification supervened. A surgeon was called upon to amputate the diseased member. Perceiving, however, that the poison had penetrated to every portion of the unfortunate man's system, he declined performing the operation, and stated that no earthly skill could save his life. After lingering in great agony, death closed the scene.

STILL ANOTHER—DEATH OF A RUSSIAN LADY FROM GLANDERS.—The awful death of Madame Palesikoff, one of the most charming amongst all that bevy of charming Russian ladies who sometimes gladden the winters of Paris, has created a terrible shock amongst the circles she so lately embellished by her presence. The unhappy lady left Paris but a short time ago, on a summer tour to Germany. While stepping from the door of the opera-house in Berlin, to gain her carriage, she let fall one of her bracelets close to the pavement. Stooping to pick it up, she noticed at the time, laughingly, that "one of the horses belonging to a carriage standing at hand, dropped his head so close to her face, that he had touched her, and left a moist kiss upon her cheek." In a few days the unfortunate lady was taken ill with that most horrible disease, glanders, and in a few day more breathed her last, in spite of the attendance of the first physicians of Berlin, and every resource to be obtained by wealth, or by the ceaseless vigilance of friends. —*Court Journal.*

In March, 1853, a messenger named Meignan, of the commune of Chemilli, consulted a quack by the name of Moyne about a discharge affecting one of his horses. Moyne, who passed in the country as formerly a pupil of the veterinary school at Alfort, and even assumed in his practice the title of veterinary surgeon, declared, after having examined Meignan's horse, that he was affected with "strangles," but that Meignan might use him and treat him without any risk of harm, and that he would answer for his recovery.

Meignan, equally simple and confiding, followed this dangerous advice. He made use of his horse, treated and groomed him according to the instructions given—in fact, was too faithful an executor of the prescriptions of a man in whom he had

15 *

placed his confidence : he would daily wipe the
nostrils of the horse clean with his pocket hand-
kerchief, lest he might be found fault with by
the authorities of the villages he was necessitated
to pass through. Such care became to him fatal.
On the 7th of April, this unfortunate messenger
fell a victim to the effects of the farcino-glander-
ous attack contracted from his horse. Some days
after his death, M. Pangoue, veterinary surgeon,
called in by the authority, pronounced that the
horse of this unfortunate man was affected with
acute glanders, and recommended accordingly his
immediate destruction. Our brethren, MM. Pangoue and Bresson, communicated to us this fact,
as another proof of the danger of empiricism.

In mentioning a similar case where two horses
were glandered, M. Pangoue says: "For the
last fortnight these horses had been treated by
the proprietor himself, who, in the course of that
time, contracted the glanders in spite of all the
precautions I had strongly urged him to take,
not doubting but that he exposed himself to great
risks. Notwithstanding one could not positively
assert the channel through which contagion had
taken place, it was very easy to suppose what the
contagious agent was, and how the glandered
virus had operated. However incomplete this
case may be deemed, especially as far as con-
cerns the unfortunate subject of contagion, do
not similar details to those I have just related,
exist in abundance, and prove in a most undeni-
able manner that human nature enjoys the sad

prerogative of contracting, through inoculation, a disease so terrible among our domestic animals, and one which veterinary science has designated under the name of glanders.—*Rec. de Med. Vet. de Sep.* 1854.

In man it is generally produced through inoculation of the matter into a wound. Whether it can be contracted by infection, through the miasmata arising from it, without actual contact of the matter, is not yet quite decided. There are, however, some grounds for believing that this disease is occasionally propagated by infection in the horse; and that the effluvia are capable of communicating some form of malignant fever, although not true glanders, to the human subject. But the matter from the abscesses or nasal cavities of human beings is capable of communicating the disease both to men and animals. A man died of glanders in St. Bartholomew's Hospital, in 1840, and the nurse who attended him inoculated her hand, and died of it also in a few days; and two kittens, which were inoculated from the nurse, became affected likewise. Moreover, the blood of a glandered horse injected into the veins of a healthy one, communicated the disease, although no abnormal appearance could be detected in it by the microscope.—*Druitt's Surgery.*

"An inquest was opened at the Guildhall, Bath, on Friday evening, September 26th, by A. H. English, Esq., the city coroner, on the body of a boy who died from glanders."—*Veterinarian,* 1862.

DEATH FROM GLANDERS. — A blacksmith,
named George Spence, residing at Aunadarragh,
and aged about forty years, was admitted into
the County Infirmary on the 27th May last, suffering from glanders.   Notwithstanding all the
efforts of medical skill, the unfortunate man
expired on the 7th ult.   This loathsome disease
must have been communicated to the deceased
by some horse which he was shoeing.   As it is
now well known that glanders is incurable, animals infected with the disease should be destroyed as soon as the first symptoms are manifested. — *Veterinary Review*, 1862.

From time to time, cases of glanders or farcy
are reported as occurring in the human subject,
but the frequency with which such reports meet
the public eye bear no relation to the actual
number of cases which are observed.   As with
several other forms of disease due to animal
poisons, there are many cases overlooked, and
never diagnosed.   We have a law referring to
glandered horses, to their use and sale, but we
can state from experience that the law is evaded.
Veterinary surgeons are not disposed to insist on
the immediate slaughter of any glandered horse
they meet with in practice.   Cases of farcy are
often much neglected, and the result is the spread
of disease.   Information has reached us of
glandered horses sold by public auction, of animals similarly affected being worked in London
omnibuses, and it is well known that glanders
has proved unusually destructive within the last

two or three years amongst the horses of our
cavalry regiments.

Ireland is no doubt the division of the United
Kingdom in which there are most cases of glanders in man and horses. In the report of the
Census Commissioners for 1851, we find the following remarks : " The number of deaths from
this cause afforded by the returns of 1841 was
but eleven; on the present occasion they amount to
one hundred and ninety-six, viz., one hundred
and sixty-eight males and twenty-eight females.
We think the magnitude in the returns for 1851
is owing, not merely to a greater knowledge, both
medical and popular, of the symptoms of the
disease, but to an increase of these affections,
and to a greater negligence on the part of persons engaged in the care of horses. Instances
have been recorded of families becoming infected
with this frightful malady from residing in the
same apartments with diseased animals. In our
report upon the statistics of disease, we have
already called attention to the subject of the increase of this affection, and pointed out the
necessity which exists for bringing infected animals under the surveillance of the police. The
seasons show the following great varieties : In
spring there died seventy-one persons from this
cause ; in summer, fifty; in winter, forty-eight ;
and in autumn, but twenty-nine." — *Veterinary
Review*, 1863.

Law respecting glandered horses in England,
reads thus : " Any person who shall sell, expose

for sale, or keep in his possession, or keep or suffer to be kept on his premises, or lead, drive, or bring in or into any street, road, or public place, any horse or beast affected with the said disease, or any disease of the like nature, knowing such horse or beast to be so affected, shall be liable to a fine not exceeding the sum of *twenty pounds* ($100), or, in default of payment, to be imprisoned for a term not exceeding *one month.*"

"Any justice or justices may order any horse or other beast affected with the said disease, together with any troughs, litter, hay, straw, or other article which he or- they shall judge likely to have been infected thereby, to be forthwith destroyed, or otherwise disposed of in such manner as he or they shall deem proper."

"In 1784, a law was enacted by the French government to prevent any one from keeping a glandered horse, under a penalty of one hundred dollars. Every animal suspected of glanders had the words 'suspected animal' impressed with green wax on his forehead; and the penalty for selling such an animal, or offering him for sale, was one hundred dollars.

"Persons having suspected animals were to report the same to the mayor, syndics of villages, or other proper authorities, under a penalty of one hundred dollars. Such horses were then inspected by experienced veterinary surgeons, appointed by the mayor or other officer, and, if found glandered, were destroyed. If only suspected, they were marked in the forehead as before described."

The foregoing is but a drop in the bucket,

compared with the recorded evidence upon the subject of glanders; time and space, however, will not permit a further extension of this subject. Our present experience in the United States of America should bring us to the level of Europe in passing laws, ordinances, on the subject of glanders. The losses already sustained by our farmers and horsemen, by the purchase of condemned and diseased government horses, amount to more than the sum realized by the government, and will go on increasing at a fearful rate.

We are told that the glandered horses of the army have been shot or destroyed, and that none are offered which are known as diseased. Half an hour in the sales-yards is more than sufficient to convince a competent judge to the contrary. It is evident to the observer that the malady exists to a great extent. Where is the fault? Is it not obvious that the officers having charge of the animals offered for sale are not competent, and do not understand the disease? How many recognised veterinary surgeons are there in the employ of the United States Government? None to speak of. Before sending a lot of horses to any place for public sale, every animal should be thoroughly inspected by the most competent surgeon, qualified as such, a graduate, a man of long experience and a practitioner, and every animal, *even suspected*, should be at once destroyed.

Very respectfully,
R. JENNINGS,
Veterinary Surgeon.
Bordentown, March 1st, 1864.

VALUABLE RECEIPTS

FROM THE PRIVATE RECEIPT-BOOK OF THE AUTHOR.

———◆◆◆———

BALLS.

R. Barb. Aloes . . . 1 dr.
    Calomel . . . . . 1 scruple.
    Linseed Meal . . -. ½ oz.

Mix with molasses. An alterative, used for diseases of the liver principally; given once a day.

R. Black Antimony . . 1 oz.
    Sulphur Flour . . 4 "
    Nitre (pulv.) . . . 1 "

Mix with honey and divide into four balls; an excellent alterative.

R. Calomel . . . . . ½ dr.
    Linseed Meal . . . 1 oz.

Mix with molasses; give at night, and follow in the morning with a purgative ball; a vermifuge.

R. Oak Bark . . . . 1 oz.
    Powdered Opium . . 1 dr.

Mix with molasses. For diarrhœa in horses.

16   (181)

R.   Ammonicum . . . . 2 drs.
      Powdered Squills . . . 1 "
      Barb. Aloes . . . . 1 "
      Linseed Meal . . . 2 "

Mix with molasses. For cough.

R.   Emetic Tartar . . . . ½ dr.
      Digitalis (pulv.) . . . ½ "
      Nit. Potassa . . . . 2 "
      Powd. Liquorice . . . 2 "

Mix with molasses. For fever in horses or cattle.

R.   Camphor Gum . . . . 2 drs.
      Nit. Potassa . . . . 3 "
      Linseed Meal . . . ½ oz.

Mix with molasses. For retention of urine.

R.   Barbadoes Aloes . . . 6 drs.
      Pulv. Ginger . . . 1 "
      " Gentian . . . 1 "

Mix with water. A purgative.

R.   Barbadoes Aloes . . . 5 drs.
      Calomel . . . . . 1 "
      Linseed Meal . . . 1 "

Mix with molasses. A good purge.

R.   Sulphate of Copper . . ½ dr.
      Sulphate of Zinc . . . ½ "
      Aniseed . . . . . 1 "
      Linseed Meal . . . 2 "

Mix with molasses. A good tonic.

R. Iron Filings . . . . . . 2 drs.
Carbonate of Potash . . 2 "
Powdered Gentian . . . 2 " .

Mix with molasses. A good tonic.

POWDERS.

R. Sulphur . . . . 1 oz.
Black Antimony . . . ½ "
Saltpetre . . . . 1 "

Mix all together. An alterative.

R. Mustard Seeds . . . . 4 oz.
Sweet Flag . . . . . 4 "
Juniper Berries . . . 2 "
Flour of Sulphur . . . 6 "
Foenigreek Seeds . . . 3 "

Mix; dose, one tablespoonful. Good in typhoid diseases.

R. Powdered Gentian . . . 2 oz.
Cascarilla (pulv.) . . . 1 "
Ginger " . . . 2 "

Mix; dose, one teaspoonful. For lost appetite.

R. Calomel . . . . 1 dr.
Sulphate of Potash . . 1 oz.
Powd. Linseed . . . . 1 "

Mix. Used in abdominal inflammation.

R.   Sulphate of Potash . . 2 oz.
      Powd. Gentian . . . . ½ "
Mix. Used in colic.

R.   Iodide of Potassa . . . 1 dr.
      Chloride of Mercury . . 1 "
      Powdered Belladonna . . ½ oz.
      White Sugar . . . . 1 "
Mix, and divide into four powders.   Put upon
the tongue for sore throat.

R.   Powdered Camphor . . 1 dr.
       "   Rhubarb   . . 2 "
       "   Opium . . . 1 "
Mix. For diarrhœa.

R.   Burnt Alum   . . . . 4 oz.
      Sulphate of Iron . . . 2 "
      Sulphate of Copper . . 1 "
      Camphor . . . . . . 2 drs.
Mix. For thrush or canker.

MIXTURES.

R.   Linseed Oil . . . . . . 1 pint.
      Croton Oil . . . . . 10 drops.
Mix. A purge.

R.   Linseed Oil . . . . . . 1 pint.
      Assafœtida . . . . . 2 drs.
Mix. Good in flatulent colic.

R. Camphor . . . . . 2 drs.
Sulphuric Ether . . . 4 "
Acetate of Ammonia . . 4 oz.

Mix. Used in typhoid diseases.

R. Quinine . . . . . . ½ dr.
Sulphuric Acid . . . . ½ "
Water . . . . . . 1 pint.

Mix, and give in warm gruel. A good tonic.

LINIMENTS.

R. Mercurial Ointment . . 1 oz.
Liquor Ammonia . . . 2 "
Camphor . . . . . 1 dr.
Sweet Oil . . . . . 4 oz.

Mix. In skin diseases.

R. Oil of Turpentine . . . 1 oz.
Tincture of Opium . . 1 "
Soap Liniment . . . . 1 "
Tincture of Capsicum . . ½ "

Mix. A good liniment.

R. Extract of Opium . . . 2 drs.
Goulard's Extract . . . 2 oz.
Water . . . . . . ½ pint.

Mix. Used in inflammatory swellings.
16*

R. Tincture of Myrrh   . . 4 oz.
    Tincture of Aloes . . . 2 "
    Water . . . . ½ pint.
Mix. For galls, sore mouth, &c.

BLISTERS.

R. Pulv. Cantharides . . . 2 drs.
    Spirits of Turpentine . . 2 "
    Powd. Euphorbium . . 1 "
    Oil Origanum . . . . 1 "
    Lard . . . . 2 oz.
Mix. A strong blister.

R. Cantharides Ointment . 2 oz.
    Tartar Emetic . . . . 1 dr.
Mix. A powerful blister.

DR. R. JENNINGS'S

HORSE AND CATTLE MEDICINES

ARE acknowledged by all who have used them to be superior to anything of the kind ever offered to the public. They are the safest, best, and cheapest preparations known; the safest, because they do not contain any deleterious drugs; the best, because they promote the general health of the animals, and protect them from attacks of disease; the cheapest, because, unlike other preparations, they do not require, when once used, to be continued longer than the desired.end is obtained.

DR. R. JENNINGS'S WORM POWDERS,
For Horses, Cattle, Sheep, &c.

The discovery of this valuable vegetable preparation was purely accidental, it never having been known as a vermifuge, and rarely used in medical practice. The success which has attended its introduction has far exceeded the most sanguine expectations of the subscribers. This Powder is safe and efficient for the removal of Worms in Horses, Cattle, Sheep, &c.

Thousands of animals die annually from the ravages of these pests, without the true cause being even suspected; especially is this the case in the young of the Mare, Cow, Sheep, and Pig. Deising, in his work on Entozoa, mentions twenty varieties of worms belonging to the Horse, nineteen to the Ox, sixteen to the Sheep, &c., Yet, veterinary writers

(187)

have mentioned but five or six of these varieties as belonging to our domestic animals, the symptoms of which have been but very imperfectly described by them.

The following symptoms, the subscribers have discovered by close observation during a period of eighteen years' practice as Veterinary Surgeons, but not all in the same animal. Each variety of worm has its own characteristic symptoms, viz.:—In bots we rarely have loss of condition, but when the bots become troublesome, colicky pains, gasping, quickened respiration, staring or haggard expression of the eye, with a strong tendency to inflammation of the bowels, will be observed; in most other varieties of worms the symptoms are debility, feebleness, sluggish movements, emaciation, staring coat, hidebound, and skin covered with scurfy blotches, rigidity of the loins, small and feeble, but slightly accelerated pulse, respiration slow, tucked-up belly, pallid appearance of the lining of the lip (a certain indication) irregular, capricious, but persistent appetite, badly digested fæces, agitation of heart and tail, and where the ascarides (fundament worms) exist, a whitish, or yellowish white substance, will be found about the fundament, indicated also by rubbing the tail.

Price Fifty Cents per Box.

DR. R. JENNINGS'S CONDITION POWDERS

Will cure Hide-bound, Mange, Surfeit, and all Eruptions of the Skin, Jaundice, Diseases of the Kidneys and Bladder, Swelled Legs, and promote a healthy condition of the system.

DR. H. JENNINGS'S TONIC POWDERS,
For Horses and Cattle.

These Powders are unequalled for promoting a healthy, glossy appearance of the coat. They are particularly recommended in Throat Distemper, Catarrhal Fever, or Typhoid Influenza (commonly called Pink Eye Distemper), Loss of Condition, Loss of Appetite, and all derangements of the Digestive Organs.

Price Fifty Cents per Box.

Prepared only by Jennings & Higgins, Veterinary Surgeons, 836 Sansom St., Phila., and Bordentown, N. J.

DR. R. JENNINGS'S COUGH POWDERS.

These Powders stand without a rival, being a certain cure for Distemper, Strangles, Chronic Cough (used in connection with Sweating Liniment), &c. The only known remedy that will successfully abate the Heaves, and in most cases, where the lungs are not involved, effect a permanent cure, if used according to directions.

Price Fifty Cents per Box.

Prepared only by Jennings & Higgins, Veterinary Surgeons, 836 Sansom St., Phila., and Bordentown, N. J.

DR. R. JENNINGS'S ANTISEPTIC POWDERS

Will cure Thrush, Canker, Scratches, &c., in the feet of Horses. It will cure Hoof Ail or Foul in the feet of Cattle. It will cure Foot Rot or Foul in the feet of Sheep; it rarely fails in the very worst cases. It will restore healthy action in unhealthy wounds, foul ulcers, &c., &c. Give it one trial and be convinced.

Price Fifty Cents.

Prepared only by Jennings & Higgins, Veterinary Surgeons, 836 Sansom St.. Phila., and Bordentown, N. J.

DR. R. JENNINGS'S ANODYNE LINIMENT

Is one of the best preparations ever offered to the public for recent injuries in man. It gives speedy relief. One trial is sufficient to convince the most skeptical, as all who have used it are willing to testify.

One dose internally will cure any ordinary case of Diarrhœa, Cramp, Colic, &c., and a few doses will cure the worst. It is not an astringent, but checks the discharge by restoring healthy action in the digestive organs. It is an excellent remedy for Sprains, Bruises, Acute Rheumatism, Sore Throat, Neuralgia, Pains in the Back, Side, or Loins, Cramp, Pains in the Limbs, Stings of Insects, Eruptions from poisonous plants, &c.

Price Fifty Cents.

Prepared only by Jennings & Higgins, Veterinary Surgeons, 836 Sansom St., Phila., and Bordentown, N. J.

DR. R. JENNINGS'S SWEATING LINIMENT.

This preparation as a counter-irritant is one of the most valuable known to Veterinary Surgeons, in all diseases of the lungs and air passages, Sore Throat or Throat Distemper, the early stages of Poll-evil or Fistula of the Withers, Enlarged Glands, Chronic Lameness, Navicula or Lameness, &c. It is unequalled for subduing Spavins, Ringbones, Splints, Exostosis, Curbs, Ossified Cartilages, or any Bony or Callous Enlargements. It does not leave any blemish, and gives universal satisfaction. Try one bottle.

Price Fifty Cents.

Prepared only by Jennings & Higgins, Veterinary Surgeons, 836 Sansom St., Phila., and Bordentown, N. J.

DR. R. JENNINGS'S POPULAR WORKS.

The Horse and his Diseases   -   -   Price, $1.75
Cattle and their Diseases   - - -   "   1.75
Sheep, Swine, Poultry, and their Diseases "   1.75

FOR SALE AT HIS OFFICES,

No. 836 Sansom St., Phila., and Bordentown, N. J.

SENT BY MAIL ON RECEIPT OF PRICE.

60,000 Copies of "The Horse and his Diseases" already sold.

DR. R. JENNINGS'S CELEBRATED HOOF OINTMENT.

The Greatest Discovery of the Age.

For Contracted Hoof, Thrush, Quarter or Toe Crack, Scratches, Corns, Fever, or Tenderness in the Feet, from Founder or other causes, Canker, Grease, &c., &c.

It softens the Hoof, restores its elasticity, prevents Contraction, Cracked Hoof, Corns, &c., and keeps the feet always in a healthy condition, when used according to directions.

Price One Dollar per Box.

Prepared only by Jennings & Higgins, Veterinary Surgeons, 836 Sansom St., Phila., and Bordentown, N. J.

KERR'S EAST INDIA LINIMENT.

The formula for preparing this valuable Liniment was first obtained from James Kerr, late Veterinary Surgeon, First Bengal Light Cavalry, by a cavalry officer in the British Army, of whom it was afterwards purchased at a heavy expense. Forty years' experience has proved it to be the very best Liniment known for Colic, Strains, Sprains, Rheumatism,

Enlarged Joints, Swelled Legs or Glands, Sprung Knees, Incipient Spavin, Strains of the Back, Capped Hock, Stifle Lameness, Blood Spavin, Curbs, and all injuries of Horses and Cattle, where an embrocation is required.

It is equally good for the following Diseases in Man: Sprains, Bruises, Rheumatism, Sore Throat, Neuralgia, Pains in the Limbs, Stings of Insects, &c.

Price One Dollar.

Prepared only by Jennings & Higgins, Veterinary Surgeons, 836 Sansom st., Phila., and Bordentown, N. J.

For Sale by Druggists and Dealers generally.

WHOLESALE AGENTS,

GALL & ROBINSON, No. 186 Greenwich Street, New York; JENKS & MIDDLETON, No. 160 North Third Street, Philadelphia, Pa.; WILLIAM H. CHADWICK, West Fourth Street, opposite City Spring, Wilmington, Delaware; and by the Proprietors, JENNINGS & HIGGINS, No. 836 Sansom Street, Philadelphia, and Bordentown, New Jersey.

NOTICE.

Persons at a distance wishing to consult DR. R. JENNINGS, regarding the diseases of Horses, Cattle, &c., can do so by letter, giving all the symptoms as accurately as possible, stating age, color, how fed, worked, &c., and enclosing a fee of $2.00.

Address JENNINGS & HIGGINS, Veterinary Surgeons No. 836 Sansom Street, Philadelphia, Pa.